WITHDRAWN

Teaching Literature ·
What Is Needed Now

HARVARD ENGLISH STUDIES   15

Teaching Literature ·
What Is Needed Now

Edited by
James Engell
and David Perkins

Harvard University Press
Cambridge, Massachusetts
London, England
1988

Library of Congress Cataloging-in-Publication Data

Teaching literature : what is needed now / edited by James Engell,
David Perkins.
    p. cm.—(Harvard English studies ; 15)
    1. Literature—Study and teaching (Higher)—United States.
    2. Criticism. I. Engell, James, 1951– . II. Perkins, David,
PN70.T35 1988
807'.1173—dc19
ISBN 0-674-86970-2 (alk. paper) (cloth)   88-11029
ISBN 0-674-86971-0 (paper)   CIP

Preface

These essays were written in response to the issue posed in the title of this volume. The editors invited eminent scholars, critics, and metacritics to reflect upon their activity as teachers. It seems important to know how people at the forefront of intellectual developments in the university perceive their teaching and its context at present. What type of society are we teaching in and for? What are the character and needs of contemporary students? What impact have the institutions of the university and the profession on our efforts? What and how should we teach? Any current group of essays on this topic would also discuss whether and how the classroom should incorporate critical theory, and it would reflect the hot controversies of the more theoretical with the less and with each other. The editors are impressed and deeply grateful that busy persons were willing to write such essays, the more so since the rewards of our profession are not doled out primarily for teaching or reflection upon it.

In extending our invitation to contribute to this volume, we did not seek to represent only a particular point of view and neither did we especially attempt to represent all that are now active within the profession. The only criterion of this kind was that the younger as well as older generations should be heard. The terms of the fund used to publish this volume require that most of the contributors have a connection, present or in the past, with Harvard University, but this connection does not in the least imply agreement. The contributors did not read each other's essays or otherwise know what they would contain. Each wrote in complete independence. It is interesting, therefore, to consider whether they share certain perceptions or beliefs.

Most of these authors seem embattled. On the one hand, the students, they say, have questionable preparation and motivation for studying literature. In freshman courses students have not read enough and cannot write adequately, as Richard Marius reports from his frontline engagement. They do not hear the sound of poetry, Hugh Kenner says, and teaching must try to impress it on them. Gregory Nagy urges that the process of reading must not be resolved into an easy technique, and uses philology in a striking way to exemplify his point. Literary seniors and graduate students tend, Nathan Scott finds, to attribute moral and spiritual authority to literature, and yet also to plunge into a premature "forensic entanglement" with their revered texts, making up their minds about the doctrine and worth of what they read without sufficiently listening to it. Scott hopes to encourage in the classroom a dialogic encounter with texts, one that would be appropriate to the pluralistic, relativistic society in which students must live. On the other hand, there is the relation of our profession to society as a whole, which does not much understand or value what we do, or love "What we have loved," as Helen Vendler applies Wordsworth, and Vendler is inclined to blame the profession for this state of affairs. James Engell expresses concern over deteriorating conditions in colleges and universities for studying literature outside the classroom.

But especially these essays are embattled in intellectual wars within the profession. As they advocate teaching a particular subject matter, or by a certain method, or with the intentions they describe, they are taking a stand amid the critical controversies of our day. Another way to make this point is to say that, with some exceptions, the writers of these essays wish to do as teachers what they also do as publishing critics. They integrate their critical or "theoretical" positions with their teaching strategies. Thus Barbara Johnson explores the relation of deconstruction to feminism both as an intellectual issue in itself and with a concern for their combination in teaching; Harry Levin defends interpretation from recent attacks on its desirability or possibility; Nathan Scott believes that instruction in literature should include a sophisticated analysis of the hermeneutic experience; tracing the changing reception of two texts, Deborah Nord shows students that their own critical reactions are as much shaped by history as are the works they react to; Robert Watson argues that, in teaching Shakespeare, the idea of the historical author, of a unitary consciousness behind the different plays, is a necessary fiction. To repeat, the essayists do not wish to conceive teaching as one activity, and research and criticism as a separate activity, each with its proper method and aim, but to unite the two. Whether this is or is not desirable—whether teaching might more appropriately be conceived as a separate art which we must also learn and practice as well as we can—might be argued, but is not argued here.

We are struck by how personal these essays are. Confession is a convention of our time, but we think the intended audience is also an explanation. Our personal experience may have a general relevance for readers who are themselves also teachers, critics, and university professionals. Watson describes encounters that helped to form his beliefs. Marius and Nord narrate their own experiences as teachers. Harry Levin writes in a personally reminiscent as well as historicizing vein, and David Perkins considers how his convictions about teaching have and have not changed over the last thirty years. What continues to motivate a teacher? From the middle of the way Shklar and Vendler testify that it must be a love of the subject matter, and Hillis Miller emphasizes a similar point, arguing that even in the classroom a teacher must be primarily oriented not toward an interchange with the students but toward the text, toward reading. The essay by Miller constitutes a dialogue of his mind with itself extending over several years.

The reader of these essays will find other elements in common. Deconstruction, whether favorably regarded or assailed, is an issue in several. So also are problems of hermeneutics. Whether or how the study of other disciplines, such as philosophy, anthropology, and history, should be incorporated with the teaching of literature is a recurrent consideration. Yet it goes without saying that the essays also and primarily disagree with each other. The disagreement is not, moreover, as among parties in a state, where opinions group around a few rallying points, but more resembles the Brownian motion of particles, in which each follows its own separate path even while colliding with others. More essays would have contributed more disagreement, as is the intellectual character of our age.

J.E.
D.P.

Contents

Beginnings

HUGH KENNER

Teaching Poetry

By chance, a student mentioned her father's long-ago habit of reciting. Exposed to his declamations, she'd known by heart portions of *The Ancient Mariner* before she could read. I don't need to tell you that she's a superior student; and why do I not need to tell you that? Because, as I think it's readily intuited, there are things for which she was not dependent on a teacher: things teachers may or may never think to impart.

She'd needed no persuading, notably, about poetry's ancient mnemonic function. Enabled by rhythm, word-clusters stick to the mind; hence Homer's Catalogue of Ships, in hexameters. Nor had anyone had to tell her how written language can engage the larynx, the mouth, the lungs, the torso, arms, hands: all that we feebly intend when we speak of "sound": a power to possess the body, alarming alike to Plato and to chartered accountants. (Possession is unacademic; it's like witchcraft.)

Students, not to mention colleagues, tend to be mystified by Robert Frost's claim that the sound of poetry is like what you hear of a conversation in the next room: a vocal tune lacking words, to which, optionally, "sense" may be fitted. Yeats's

'I am of Ireland,
And the Holy Land of Ireland,

3

> And time runs on,' cried she.
> 'Come out of charity
> Come dance with me in Ireland.'[1]

makes, as the late Basil Bunting liked to point out, very little in the way of paraphrasable sense. A Canto of *The Divine Comedy,* at the other extreme, makes a great deal; but
Dante's undertaking, it's grown hard for us to realize, was not
so much finding verse for his sense as working sense into his
verse.

The *terza rima,* that was primary: an initial, encompassing
choice. Then, over and over, episodes will have been shaped
by a phatic and acoustic intuition, itself shaped and set free to
gather words. Thus at the end of *Purgatorio XXVI,* the shaping
decision was to let Arnaut speak his own language. Provençal
therefore; and, shifted from their daily Italian, readers' tongues
would dance differently. So, some forty words: and from what
Provençal zone? Dante will have groped toward a rich patch
dominated by the "-or" which governs so many prime words in
that language: *amor, cor, flor.*

> Ieu sei Arnaut, que pl*or* e vau cantan;
> consiros vei la passada fol*or,*
> e vei jausen lo j*or*n, qu'esper, denan.

Then the great line that caught T. S. Eliot's ear—"Ara vos
prec, per acquella valor"—with its balancing or initial, medial,
terminal:

> *Ara* vos prec, p*er a*quella val*o*r.

The last rhyme, of course, is "dolor," and we are left to recall
some words from a former life that Arnaut doesn't utter here:
amor, cor, flor. No love, no hearts, no flowers. But alike, the

1. William Butler Yeats, "I Am of Ireland," from *The Collected Poems of
W. B. Yeats* (New York: Macmillan, 1956). Reprinted by permission of the
publishers: Copyright 1933 by Macmillan Publishing Company, renewed 1961
by Bertha Georgie Yeats; and A. P. Watt Ltd. on behalf of Michael B. Yeats
and Macmillan London Ltd.

words that are heard and the words that aren't will have come from the way Dante wanted the lines to feel when you uttered them.

Pound, composing, intoned inarticulate sounds; Wordsworth shouted nascent passages aloud to help himself shape them; Keats prized things proven "on the pulses"; Sam Johnson made his verses pacing up and down. So *physical* an art; and D. H. Lawrence came at it from the right direction when he got his Croydon pupils all chanting in unison, "The As*syr*ian came *down* like the *wolf* on the *fold,*" though from neighboring classrooms there were complaints of the din.

And here we are, facing a roomful of postadolescents, seated before books all open to be looked at. They are lookers. They "scan" headlines, glance at T-shirts. Their eye-culture is silent, abstract. Such as spell securely are bothered by funny spelling: "Busie old foole, unruly Sunne." Compassionate anthology-editors "modernize." That's one stumbling-block removed.

These are what Yeats designated as "reading-books," a phrase inconceivable before our classroom era: books for opening when "reading" is to be the hour's formal act; otherwise to stay firmly shut. Look into one of them, for instance the Oxford *Anthology,* and be instructed by its fine print that Prospero's "dark backward and abysm of time" means "dark abyss of time past," as Shakespeare might have written in the first place if he'd had the wit. Or try the Norton, and watch its wrestle with Arnold's line about the Sea of Faith, that once

> Lay like the folds of a bright girdle furled.

This difficult line means, in general, that at high tide the sea envelopes the land closely. Its forces are "gathered" up (to use Wordsworth's term for it) like the "folds" of bright clothing ("girdle") which have been compressed ("furled").

Lord, Lord, yes, mercy, we do need air, air. That is *not* a way to teach poetry, enforcing as it does whatever suspicion that poets just can't talk straight. More pertinent to adduce the shortage of rhymes with which English confronts a poet when he wants to close his cadence with that satisfying mouthful, "world." In a similar difficulty, Milton, even, had to settle for letting undersea bones be "hurled,"and we may conclude that Arnold came off pretty well.[2]

Yet we must start from the book, which after all does offer something to start from. Since Gutenberg, our first impression of every poem has been the look of it. (It has not, perhaps, been pondered sufficiently that in Sidney's time a Sonnet was a poem that sat well on an octavo page.) You can tell a lot about *In Memoriam* simply by looking: page after page of chastely measured dolor, in quatrains formally grouped under Roman numerals. That is no primitive cry; that is *measured* grief, and, by Victorian custom, measured at length. (The Queen's decades of formal widowhood would be notorious.)

We can learn, then, from looking, and may as well learn to look. (What's learned by looking at "The Red Wheelbarrow"? At "Dover Beach"?) If we're reading one poet at length, each poem's look on the page may evoke a personal code. The glance that identifies the Yeats *ottava rima* stanza prepares us for its special ceremonies. (If, as seems likely, he first used it for "Ancestral Houses," then in his mind it's tied to courtly Italy; that helps locate "The Municipal Gallery Revisited.")

Next, the plunge into sound's physicalities. Miss A, could you let us hear the first four lines? Miss A *loquitur:*

busy old fool unruly sun why dost thou thus through windows and through curtains call on us must to thy motions lovers seasons run.

There are teachers who can make that tactic work; I can't. Arriving at something better without leaving Miss A to feel dashed presents more complications than I enjoy. Generally, I read the lines out myself, with a force propelled by a heritage of Welsh preachers. Whatever I'm teaching, "The Sunne Rising" or "Canto XX" or *Ulysses,* I do much reading aloud. Whether it is exemplary reading or not Sir Laurence Olivier might well dispute; but it does have two advantages. It slows down the

---

2. Not that all annotation is impertinent. For the plight of a student who imagines "the naked shingles of the world" as somehow affixed to its roof, the Norton's gloss, "Beaches covered with pebbles," is as quick a fix as any. W. H. Auden's way of teaching Americans *Lycidas* was to have them look up every one of its first fifty words in the *O.E.D.,* where they'd find as much to instruct them about "yet" as about "laurels."

pace at which the students encounter the words. And it nudges them, continually, from eye to ear. Maybe, even, they parody me in the dorms. If so, they're beginning to vocalize.

Time enough, when they've gained some physical possession of the poem, to investigate effects of tone and diction: Donne's Sun as Peeping Tom, no, as Peeping Polonius; the special Ptolemaic usage of "center" and "sphere"; the piquant swagger of such pedantries in a love poem. Some students—much depends on the class—will be glad to hear about the great Provençal tradition of the *alba:* the rebuke to love's enemy, daylight. That's behind Donne (who knew no Provençal), and so is much else; but slowly, slowly; the great thing to get used to is poetry's slow way of letting meaning *emerge.* We'll not compress into an hour what can take centuries; much has still to emerge from Shakespeare.

Though in an hour the process can sometimes be glimpsed. Here's a seeming opacity:

> Sound slender, quasi tinnula,
> Ligur' aoide: Si no'us vei, Domna don plus me cal,
> Negus vezer mon bel pensar no val."
> Between the two almond trees flowering,
> The viel held close to his side;
> And another: "s'adora."
> "Possum ego naturae
> non meminisse tuae!" Qui son Properzio ed Ovidio.[3]

The opening of "Canto XX" disentangles itself but slowly from the sounding voice. "Sound slender"—when you *sound* it—takes up at least much time as "To be or not to be, that is the question" and serves, what is more, to upset most received notions of scansion. Back somewhere, in the minds of some students, there will be a supreme friction between what you must do to utter those two words and what appeared on some former teacher's list of "feet." But "Sóund slénder"; two *kinds* of "long" syllable; and gauge the duration of that pause between them. Then "quasi tinnula"—quick, and like (so its words say)

3. Ezra Pound, "Canto XX," from *Cantos of Ezra Pound* (New York: New Directions, 1970).

a little bell. Move on, to the intricacies of Provençal flowing
into English; I'll mark but one set of the assonances—

> Si no'us vei, Domna don *pl*us me *cal,*
> Negus vezer mon *bel* pensar no *val."*
> Between the two *al*mond trees *fl*owering,
> The v*iel* h*el*d *cl*ose to his side

—and affirm that by the time they've experienced that on their
tongues they've moved closer than deconstruction will ever bring
them to Eliot on poetry experienced before it is understood.
Understanding, an available boon; yes, it does come; but after.

For observe that, with 31 of its 48 words drawn from alien
lexicons, that wonderful vignette will reach monolingual ears as
the pure interwoven senseless sound out of which, I'm asserting,
much poetry gets drawn. If you'll not reject it out of incom-
prehension you can start tracing its weave. Meanings, as they
get supplied, will fit in; "Ligur' aoide," the "clear sound" of
the Sirens; "Si no'us vei," Bernart de Ventadorn, on a later
page rendered by Pound,

> And if I see her not,
> no sight is worth the beauty of my thought;

"s'adora," a tag from Cavalcanti, where an image of his lady,
he says, is adored. As you gather sense, you gather the way a
poet puts sense in, careful never to damage the tune. The strong
poem survives its sense. There are words in Homer that Hesiod
didn't understand; conceivably words Homer, even, was simply
chanting: inherited epithets custom had rendered sacred. Take
boōpis, where we've been taught to read "ox-eyed," Hera of
the big brown eyes. But the word can say "ox-faced." Had that
goddess migrated from Egypt? And how did Homer imagine
her?

You don't have to "understand" everything you read; and
you'll never understand it wholly. That's one permanent lesson.

Such is one way in, and it does take time. The more students,
the more time, and some who signed up just to fulfil "the English
requirement" will have been resourceful in finding something
else to drift away to. In one graduate seminar I returned to
"Canto XX" so frequently an earnest student asked if we couldn't

have more "discussion." She now professes at Y, where they doubtless "discuss."

The Lord knows what they do here and there. My wife, in college, found herself in a class where a whole academic quarter went to "The Windhover." You may be sure they *discussed* it. Then there's "Ozymandias," which students are apt to encounter in grade school, then again in junior high, then yet again in the freshman survey: at, the jargon goes, ripening levels of maturity. By freshman-survey time they're prompted to apply it to Richard Nixon, or perhaps to all three Kennedys, as though it were a *New York Times* editorial, the political being the securest American area of judgment, adjoined as it is to the Puritan moral domain. The awkward question, why then Shelley didn't write it like a *New York Times* editorial, gets finessed, and his fine diminuendo goes unremarked:

> Nothing beside remains. Round the decay
> Of that colossal wreck, boundless and bare
> The lone and level sands stretch far away.

That'd not get past a *Times* copyeditor, who'd demand more pointed relevance. (And how, pray tell, are sands "lone"?)

In our century we have the advantage of the poets' very voices, preserved. You can hear (in two versions) Yeats chanting "Innisfree," the way he annoyed a Boston lady so much she demanded to know why he read in that extraordinary fashion. On being told that he read as all true poets since Homer had read, she demanded to know how he knew that *Homer* had read in that extraordinary fashion. He replied that the ability of the man justified the presumption. Or you can hear Parson Eliot's peculiar dead intonation of "tubers," or Stevens reading "An Ordinary Evening in New Haven," carefully, like the fine print on a surety bond, or Basil Bunting doing *Briggflatts* in the authentic Northumbrian, a phase of his lifelong protest against the BBC (for which he once read Wordsworth's *Michael,* using the vowels and burrs he shared with Wordsworth and, he said, with Spenser and Swinburne). Hearing such things can be a beginning of wisdom, for students uncowed by the acoustic presence. One thing the poet does know about his verse is how it sounded before it had all its words to distract us.

Yes, tape-players and all that. Gadgetry in the classroom may merely distract. A good discreet A/V aide can help. Ideally you'd just gesture to bring on the Voice. And let students not suppose it's the *only*, the Authorized Voice. The voice we hear sounding all poems must ultimately be our own.

With the right poet, though, it's enhancing to hear what the poet heard. From time to time Basil did *Briggflatts* in public, all the way from the unchallengeable opening line,

> Brag, sweet tenor bull

through the intricate middle, for instance,

> As the player's breath warms the fipple the tone clears.
> It is time to consider how Domenico Scarlatti
> condensed so much music into so few bars
> with never a crabbed turn or congested cadence,
> never a boast or a see-here; and stars and lakes
> echo him and the copse drums out his measure,
> snow peaks are lifted up in moonlight and twilight
> and the sun rises on an acknowledged land

—all the way to the muted end:

> Who,
> swinging his axe
> to fell kings, guesses
> where we go?[4]

Those were ceremonious occasions, for which he wanted the full Persian ritual. In Persia the bard would sip at need strong wine, poured him by a lissome girl, the *saqhi*. Away from Persia, it was necessary to make do. Once, in Orono, Maine, a chubby ten-year-old was conscripted to play *saqhi*. How was she to manage not to fidget? And pretend to adore the poetry? And be videotaped to boot? She *did not want to do this*. But in adolescence, in a school essay, she could say how it had been:

It was his voice, raspy, deep, purring, falling like water, that carried me away. . . . We were alone, he and I, in poetry . . . a self-sufficient unit that read poetry and poured wine.

4. Basil Bunting, *Briggflatts,* from *Collected Poems* (Oxford: Oxford University Press, 1978).

As it turned out, the reading lasted over one and a half hours. For me it was over in minutes . . . I did not understand much of Basil's vocabulary, topics or historical allusions. His images utterly lost me. I did not know who he was. Yet we experienced something special. We travelled via poetry to places and images far away.

Now a collegian, she'd put that more maturely. No hurry. And some day she'll get around to reading *Briggflatts*. But that evening she learned the gist of how poetry works.

HELEN VENDLER

What We Have Loved

I choose as my text Wordsworth's vow at the end of *The Prelude:*

> What we have loved,
> Others will love, and we will teach them how.[1]

I would wish for all of us, scholars, a steady memory of the time when we were not yet scholars—before we knew what research libraries or variorum editions were, before we had heard any critical terms, before we had seen a text with foot-notes. It was in those innocent days that our attachment to literature arose—from reading a novel or a poem or from seeing a play. In every true reading of literature in adult life we revert to that early attitude of entire receptivity and plasticity and innocence before the text. I once heard Northrop Frye maintain this view in a lecture; it is only later, he said, after the immersion in reading, that we turn to debate, query, or commentary. His listeners at that time disputed his remark, arguing that they were scholars and could not forget, as they reread *Hamlet,* its textual and critical problems. The discussion ended in a stale-

1. This essay was delivered at Houston, Texas, as the 1980 MLA Presidential Address.

13

mate, with neither side conceding. To my mind, if I understood him correctly, Frye was right. Though the state of reading, like that of listening to a piece of music, is one of intense attention, it is not one of scholarly or critical reflection. It is a state in which the text works on us, not we on it. In that state, scholarship, criticism, and theory are suspended, though, paradoxically, everything we know and are is unreflexively brought to bear; and the hesitations, pleasures, and perplexities we encounter and absorb in that state are the material, as we bring them to consciousness, for all subsequent intellectual reflection. It is this state of intense engagement and self-forgetfulness that we hope our students will come to know. From that state, at least ideally, there issue equally the freshman essay, the senior thesis, the scholarly paper on prosody, the interdisciplinary paper on social thought and literature, the pedagogical paper on compositional structure, the variorum edition, and the theoretical argument. No matter how elementary or how specialized the written inquiry, it originated in problems raised by human submission to, and interrogation of, a text.

We all know well, and therefore feel no need to explain, the connection between our first reading and writing as students and our scholarly reading and writing now. But the public in general, and even some of our administrators, know us less well than we know ourselves. They do not understand what we do as scholars and critics; nor do they understand how that advanced study differs from what we do in the classroom. They assume that what we write in journals for an audience of peers is what we say to young students in our courses; and consequently they suspect (in the way they would not in the case of a neurologist or a particle physicist speaking to peers) that we are engaged in "overspecialization." They would, like the people in Marianne Moore's gibe, prefer us to write "in plain American that cats and dogs can read." In explaining ourselves—and our more difficult writers, too—to such critics, we must think back not only to our own first principles but also to our own experience as timid readers and students before we became professionals. But it is not the words we address to one another that will reach the general public and give them a truer idea of us; nor will critical books reach them. We have one chief way of reaching that public, and that is in our classrooms. The idea of us that they glean from their first classroom experience is often an unhappy one: and that is why I have taken up here the question of how best to teach others how to love what we have loved. Since most people do not love what we love, and will not in their lifetimes love it, we are easily discouraged. As teachers of English and foreign languages, we first meet our pupils in freshman English or in freshman language classes— and these students are often there involuntarily. We complain that the musicologist does not have to teach every freshman to compose music; the art historian does not have to teach everyone to paint; but the English teacher is expected to teach everyone to write. We meet our students in the least winning way, calling on them to practice an art or a language they are no more trained in than they are in composing quartets or painting in oils. It by no means follows, as we know, that to be able to speak one's native language means that one can write it; one can sing songs without being able to score a note. Our students necessarily experience uncertainty, and even shame, as we ask them, in elementary English and language classes, to confront and overcome their inhibitions of expression in their own or a foreign language. In the best possible result, we liberate them into a satisfying written speech. But it is not easy for all beginning students to find happiness in what Dickinson called "This consent of Language / This loved Philology."

The concern we all feel for our students' difficulty in writing leads to different theories of how best to lead them to a true ease in writing, and we are, within ourselves, divided on this subject. We have forgotten, I think, how unnatural writing is; most people, historically, have had little need for writing in life and have got along, after their few years of schooling ended, with speech as their medium of social exchange. Writers—easy and natural writers—have always been, first of all, readers. Just as spoken language is absorbed by the ear, so written language has to be learned from the pages of writers—from writers who wrote for the love of the art. Our composition classes, on the whole, neglect this elementary truth. But there is another reason, as well, for having our composition students read "art writings" rather than journalism or "model essays" or—deplorably—examples of student writing. That second reason has to do with what the American public are to think of us.

The adolescent young are much more likely to find the solace, insight, and truth they have a right to expect from us as "humanists" in poems, plays, stories, fables, and tales than they are to find these gifts in the exercises and models of elementary classes in composition and language. The divorce of composition from the reading of powerful imaginative writing is our greatest barrier to creating an American public who understand what we love. They think we love the correct use of "lie" and "lay" or the agreement between subject and predicate—and so we do; but those are not our only loves, or even our first loves. We love uneducated poets like Whitman; we love poets who cannot spell, like Keats and Yeats. If we are given half the youth of America for a term or a year, for thirty or sixty hours of freshman English, can we not give them *The Book of Ruth* or *The Song of Myself* or Chekhov as well as warnings about dangling participles? If writing is to reading as speaking is to listening, can we not hope to advance on the front of composition by providing reading's indispensable literary education of the untrained ear and eye as well as writing's training of the uncertain hand? Can we not, in foreign languages, include, even at the earliest levels, some simple genuine literature, myths or parables, so that the hungry sheep are not fed only pattern drills? There are classes in which these admirable things are done; we need to diffuse their example, if we are to correct the prevalent impression of us as inhibiting pedants with an obsessive relation to "correctness"—whether correctness of usage or correctness of pronunciation.

Wordsworth, early in *The Prelude,* speaks of youth as a time "When every hour brings palpable access / Of knowledge, when all knowledge is delight" (II, 286–87). If our students, in their first acquaintance with departments of English and foreign languages, experience too little of that delight at the access of knowledge, it is because the best delights we have to offer—those of literature—have somehow not been included in our first courses for students—courses that are often our last chance to reach them. If we could awaken in our beginning students, in their first year, the response that they can all feel to the

human story told in compelling ways, we would begin to form
a general public who approve of what we are and what we do.
After all, in their first course in music they hear wonderful
scores; in their first course in art they see wonderful paintings—
and their minds should receive equal stimulus from us. That is
the first step in teaching people how to love what we have
loved.

But, as scholars, we also teach at a more complicated level;
we love, beyond philology and composition and literature, the
work of scholarship, by which we mean accurate evidence on
literary matters. We are engaged in teaching others—our more
advanced students—how to love what we love in the discipline
of scholarship: how to prize the exact edition over the inade-
quate one; how to estimate the dispassionate presentation of
fact over tendentious argument; how to value concision and
clarity over obscurity and evasiveness; how to appreciate a new
critical vocabulary when it brings new energy or insight into our
world. It was as graduate students that we ourselves first reached,
in ignorance, for editions and commentaries, trying to understand Marvell or Hölderlin; we all recall adopting certain critics
or scholars as especially congenial models, whom we could admire and imitate if not ever equal. We must make it clearer, to
those both within and outside university life who do not understand what we do, how strong is the chain of transmission
of scholarship, by insubordination as well as filiation, from one
generation to the next. Love is shown, as Harold Bloom has
made us recognize, as much by revolutionary reaction and reap-
propriation as by gratitude and imitation. The attentiveness of
scholarship to the most minute aspects, as well as to the grander
ones, of literature is an instance, to quote Wordsworth once
more, of the "most watchful power of love," which leaves "a
register / Of permanent relations, else unknown" (*The Prelude*
ɪɪ, 291–93).

If we succeed at all in teaching others, from freshmen to
graduate students, to love what we have loved, we hope that
some of them will become the teachers who will replace us—
and that they will teach out of love, and write out of love, when
they do write. It is now more often than not administrators,
seeking to make even smaller the eye of the needle through

which the young must pass for tenure, who begin to make quantitative demands for publication, invoking a standard defensible perhaps in research institutions but corrupting and fraudulent when applied universally. We allow surgeons to operate and not write; we allow lawyers to plead cases and not write; cannot we allow teachers in colleges to teach and not write? There is no need to expect all teachers to be writers. Writing is a different profession from teaching, a different profession even from scholarly research and discovery, a different profession from the profession of critical thinking. Writing demands different impulses, different talents, a different temperament. Writing not done out of love will never serve to teach others how to love what we have loved.

We must, I think, come to some consensus about what we do love and what we wish to teach others to love. One of the forms our recent discouragement has taken is our despair over the curriculum: if students will not enroll for a course in Spanish drama of the Golden Age or for a course in Milton, how, we wonder, are we to teach them what we love? The answer will be different on each campus; but the answer is certainly not the abandoning of all pre-twentieth-century authors. With the partial dissolution of the historically organized curriculum, many departments of English have resigned themselves to offering courses in film, science fiction, and contemporary American writing. But more imaginative departments have invented courses, centered on themes or styles, that include a range of authors from Chaucer to Faulkner. And departments of English and foreign langauges alike can press for, and participate in, core courses that will restore to our students, so unjustly deprived of a knowledge of cultural riches, a sense of how many great authors there are to know.

It remains, after all, mysteriously true that students can develop enthusiasm even for arcane materials mediated by a teacher of sufficient talent. The best guarantee of having Milton taught is having a gifted teacher of Milton in the department. If the authors we love are not being taught, it is not our students' fault: it is our own. The angels, as a poet remarked, keep their ancient places; the greatest authors keep their ancient sustaining powers, too; our students will love those authors if we can find ways to bring students and authors together, even if under different rubrics from those historical or generic ones on which we ourselves were reared.

We love, we must recall, two things centrally: one is literature, but the other, equally powerful, is language. In our eagerness to convey all of literature to our students, we create courses offering works in translation: it would not do, we say, for our students to be ignorant of Homer because they have not learned Greek or for them to miss Dostoevsky because they have no Russian; we would be sorry not to have them read the *Odyssey* or *The Idiot*. There is a conspiracy, a benevolent one, to pretend that after a course given in translation, we know the *Odyssey* or *The Idiot*. We do, in part, but not wholly; and I think we must make much clearer to ourselves and to our students what it is we do know, and what we do not know, from such reading in translation. We will then know better what we are teaching in the opposite situation, when we are teaching works in the language in which they were written. If we teach Dickens in English in the same terms in which we teach Dostoevsky in translation—as a large matter of themes and social concerns and governing imagery—then we are not doing justice to what we love in our native language. We might just as well be teaching an Italian translation of Dickens. Our students need to love not just Shakespeare's characters but Shakespeare's language, not just Keats's sentiments but Keats's English—that English which he thought should be kept up. And they need to love not just Dante's visionary structures but his sumptuously varied Italian. We have given too little thought to the teaching of the language of literature; it is a separate language, with its own rules. The American pragmatic and moral tradition of literary pedagogy tends to make the literature class a class dealing (often sentimentally) with ethics or sociology or history or religion rather than a class investigating an incomparable and idiosyncratic voice, which speaks a language so distinctively its own that we can identify it, after a sentence or two, as the language of Keats or Dante. If the recent emphasis on the intertextuality of literature—that commerce which poems have with each other—helps to redress the wrongs literature has suffered at the hands of eager or sentimental moralists, it will not come amiss; and it will make more precise what it is that we love in literature.

It is perhaps true that we all love different things in literature, or love literature for different reasons. Some love the literature of a specific topic—literature about God, or literature about history. Some love the literature of a particular age, and they become specialists in a given period. Some love the writing of a single author, and they become our Proustians or our Shakespeareans. Some love the literature of puzzle, some the literature of philosophical argument, some the literature of rhetoric, some the literature of social reform. Because of our inevitable biases of training and predilection, reformations and counterreformations spring up among us. Fashions in literary discourse are themselves harmless and entertaining—and even necessary, lest one good custom should corrupt the world; it seems idle to hope for a single orthodoxy. It is certainly more instructive to our students to find teachers coming at literature from many vantage points than to be subjected to a single vision; and the most useful critical truth a student can learn is that a piece of literature yields different insights depending on the questions put to it. The best argument for a critical position is the serenity with which it is practiced, not the defensiveness that it exhibits. If we remember our common love of our texts, we can afford to be hospitable to critical difference and serene in our own affinities.

Finally, we must give some thought, if we are to preserve what we love, to our present and our future. In recent years we have been urged—by the Rockefeller Commission on the Future of the Humanities, for example—to make common cause with the other disciplines grouped loosely together under the label "the humanities"—philosophy, religion, history, musicology, art history, the classics. There is no reason why we should not find strength in union, especially for the purpose of lobbying, since administrations and foundations understand strength better than delicacy. But in such necessary joint undertakings, we are more bound than ever to recall our own separateness from other disciplines. National literatures, and the languages that are their bases, do not translate easily into supranational or interdisciplinary realms. Each language is stubbornly itself, and it never entirely yields up its being except to native speakers; literature is a dense nest of cultural and linguistic meanings inaccessible to the casual passerby. Even more, each of our great authors is unique: what is true of Austen is not true of Lawrence; what is true of Ronsard is not true of Racine. A general interdisciplinary Poloniuslike religious-historical-philosophical-cultural overview will never reproduce that taste on the tongue—as distinctive as alum, said Hopkins—of an individual style. And though we are urged, by an authority as congenial as the anthropologist Clifford Geertz, to see art (as he has seen the art of Bali) as one cultural manifestation among many, intimately linked to the way a culture manifests itself in government and in the private order, we must reply that we prize not something we call "Renaissance literature" but *King Lear,* not "the Victorian temper" but *In Memoriam,* not modernism but *Ulysses;* and what we prize in them is precisely what does *not* exist elsewhere in the culture of which they form a part, their own idiosyncrasy. We love in *King Lear* precisely what distinguishes it from *Hamlet* or *Doctor Faustus,* the quality that makes it not simply a Renaissance tragedy, not simply a Shakespearean play, but the single and unrepeatable combination of elements we call *King Lear.* It is from the experience of one or two such works that we were all led to the place where we now are, and it is from that original vision—of the single, unduplicatable, compelling literary object—that we must always take our final strength in university life and public life alike, whatever combinatorial tactics prudence may occasionally recommend.

If the present state of what we love is precarious, and its future uncertain, we can take some comfort in Yeats's cold and true words:

> But is there any comfort to be found?
> Man is in love and loves what vanishes,
> What more is there to say?[2]

Whole civilizations, as Yeats reminds us, have been put to the sword. Living languages have become dead languages; some

---

2. William Butler Yeats, "Nineteen Hundred and Nineteen," ll. 41–43, from W. B. Yeats, *The Poems of W. B. Yeats,* ed. Richard J. Finneran (New York: Macmillan, 1983), p. 208.

languages have vanished before they could be recorded. Whole literary genres have disappeared. Literature has passed from being oral to being written. Beautiful forms of writing, like the hieroglyphics, have gone from the face of the earth. For all our efforts in the classroom and in public life to convey what we love, we may be in fact witnessing, as some have argued, a change in our culture from the culture of the letter to the culture of the image. In that case, reading will persist, like listening to chamber music, as the refuge of a comparative few. Though we can scarcely envisage a time when the best-loved texts of our various mother tongues will have become obsolete, we have only to think of the concerns of the medieval university to realize how completely its curriculum has disappeared. Ours may be no more permanent.

What we can be certain of is the persistence of art, and of literary art, in some form, since in every culture, as Wordsworth said, the mind of man becomes by its aesthetic inventions, "A thousand times more beautiful than the earth / On which he dwells." For Wordsworth, as he closed *The Prelude,* this was the highest possible compliment to the mind, that it should be, by its aesthetic capacity, more beautiful than this frame of things, the earth. The mind of man is "above this frame of things . . . / In beauty exalted"; and that beauty of the mind was, to Wordsworth as to us, chiefly visible in that "transparent veil" of words which, in literature, both embodied and transformed the things of this world. Besides the great Nature of the physical world, there is, says Wordsworth, a "great Nature that exists in works / Of mighty Poets." It is that great poetic Nature which we are charged to transmit to our students and to the larger public, who need to understand both what we do and what literature does. Literature shows us the world again so that we recognize it, says Wordsworth; at the same time, literature pours a transforming light on the world, investing it—by bestowing on it insight, shape, and concentration—with a glory not its own:

>   Visionary power
>   Attends the motions of the viewless winds,
>   Embodied in the mystery of words;
>   There, darkness makes abode, and all the host

> Of shadowy things work endless changes there,
> As in a mansion like their proper home.
> Even forms and substances are circumfused
> By that transparent veil with light divine,
> And, through the turnings intricate of verse,
> Present themselves as objects recognized,
> In flashes, and with glory not their own.
>
> *(The Prelude* v, 595–605)

Wordsworth's vocabulary of a divine veil of verse, clothing with an unfamiliar glory the objects of the earth, is perhaps not the vocabulary we might now use. One of our own modern poets thought it truer to say of his *Collected Poems* that they were like the geography teacher's terrestrial globe—an exact representation, point for point, of the planet, only smaller. He called the book containing his poems "The Planet on the Table" and said that he was glad he had written his poems:

> They were of a remembered time,
> Or of something seen that he liked.
>
> .   .   .   .   .
>
> It was not important that they survive.
> What mattered was that they should bear
> Some lineament or character,
>
> Some affluence, if only half-perceived,
> In the poverty of their words,
> Of the planet of which they were part.[3]

Wordsworth thought words conferred divine light; Stevens apologizes for their poverty in reproducing the riches of sensation and memory. We recognize the truth of both assertions and alternately dwell on one or the other. When we emphasize the creating light in the mystery of words, we ponder the power of language itself in its aesthetic use; when we feel the poverty of language we emphasize the affluence of the planet—its sights, societies, institutions, concepts, and events—reflected in literature—our best mirror, if a limited one. We advance on two fronts, one chiefly aesthetic, the other chiefly mimetic; each,

3. Wallace Stevens, "The Planet on the Table," ll. 2–3 and 10–15, from *The Collected Poems of Wallace Stevens* (New York: Alfred A. Knopf, 1968) p. 532.

under hostile glances, can appear unworthy, but we know that both are necessary and that we love in literature both its mimetic powers and its inward-turning self-possession.

We also advance on the two fronts of the extensive and the intensive: there is a place, in teaching others to love what we love, for the rapid survey as well as for the course on one author. Our students come to us from secondary school having read no works of literature in foreign languages and scarcely any works of literature in their own language. The very years, between twelve and eighteen, when they might be reading rapidly, un-critically, rangingly, happily, thoughtlessly, are somehow dis-sipated without cumulative force. Those who end their education with secondary school have been cheated altogether of their literary inheritance, from the Bible to Robert Lowell. It is no wonder that they do not love what we love; we as a culture have not taught them to. With a reformed curriculum beginning in preschool, all children would know about the Prodigal Son and the Minotaur; they would know the stories presumed by our literature, as children reading Lamb's *Tales from Shakespeare* or Hawthorne's *Tanglewood Tales* once knew them. We can surely tell them the tales before they can read Shakespeare or Ovid; there are literary forms appropriate to every age, even the youngest. Nothing is more lonely than to go through life uncompanioned by a sense that others have also gone through it, and have left a record of their experience. Every adult needs to be able to think of Job, or Orpheus, or Circe, or Ruth, or Lear, or Jesus, or the Golden Calf, or the Holy Grail, or An-tigone in order to refer private experience to some identifying frame or solacing reflection.

I do not mean, by emphasizing the great tales of our inherited culture, to minimize the local and the ethnic. Literary imagi-nation is incurably local. But it is against the indispensable background of the general literary culture that native authors assert their local imaginations. Our schools cannot afford to neglect either resource. Nor do I mean, by dwelling on the narrative content of literature, to ignore the difference between a retelling like Lamb's *Tales from Shakespeare* and Shakespeare himself. If we give our children the tales, in abridged or adapted form, it is because we hope they will then come to the real thing—the *Nibelungenlied* or the Gospels or Homer—with some sense of intimacy and delighted recognition, rather than with a sense of the unfamiliar and the daunting. And if they know the story in one form, a simple one, and meet it later in another, more complicated form, they are bound to be curious about the differences of linguistic embodiment, and there literary interest, and literary appreciation, can begin.

It is not within our power as scholars to reform the primary and secondary schools, even if we have a sense of how that reform might begin. We do have it within our power, I believe, to reform ourselves, to make it our own first task to give, especially to our beginning students, that rich web of assocations, lodged in the tales of majority and minority culture alike, by which they could begin to understand themselves as individuals and as social beings. We must give them some examples of literature, suited to their level of reading, in which these tales have an indisputably literary embodiment. All freshman English courses, to my mind, should devote at least half their time to the reading of myth, legend, and parable; and beginning language courses should do the same. We owe it to ourselves to teach what we love in our first, decisive encounter with our students and to insist that the freedom to write is based on a freedom of reading. Otherwise we misrepresent ourselves, and we deprive our students. Too often, they go away, disheartened by our implicit or explicit criticism of their speech and writing in English or in a foreign language; and we go away disheartened by our conviction that we have not in that first year engaged their hearts or their minds; and both parties never see each other again. And the public, instead of remembering how often, in later life, they have thought of the parable of the talents, or the loss of Eurydice, or the sacrifice of Isaac, or the patience of Penelope, or the fox and the grapes, or the minister's black veil, remember the humiliations of freshman English or long-lost drills in language laboratories. We owe it to ourselves to show our students, when they first meet us, what we are; we owe their dormant appetites, thwarted for so long in their previous schooling, that deep sustenance that will make them realize that they too, having been taught, love what we love.

Interpreting Interpreters

HARRY LEVIN

The Crisis
of Interpretation

"Nowadays," a senior colleague once said to me, obviously quite a while ago, "you young fellows seem to be going in for interpretation." A respected professor of English at a reputable university, he was benign enough to muffle his intimation of disapproval. He himself had expended most of his scholarly energies over the attribution of authorship—which lines were whose—in the collaboration of Beaumont and Fletcher. A closely related problem, that of identifying Fletcher's interpolations in one or two of Shakespeare's later plays, had vainly exhausted London's Shakespeare Society during the nineteenth century, and has yet to be convincingly solved by the current practitioners of stylometrics. But such considerations would not have detracted from the professional security of my interlocutor's position, since he had been seeking external facts about the texts he worked with, even though the way he had been working strained them with untenable conjectures. His admonition spoke for a positivistic orthodoxy, long but no longer so tightly entrenched, and lately feeling challenged by the sort of upstart to whom he found himself talking. Paradigms, as they have been envisaged for us by Thomas Kuhn, those "disciplinary matrices" which set and frame our intellectual problems, are no less encompassing in the arts than in the sciences. And these had been

29

changing rapidly at that moment, as they seem to be again today.

If the moving spirit of that old order was George Lyman Kittredge at Harvard, I could claim the transitory privilege of having been among the last of his students. Elsewhere I have paid my respects and noted my reservations. Prior and better disciples had acted as his apostles, and had spread the gospel at other American universities: notably J. M. Manly at Chicago, J. S. P. Tatlock at Berkeley, Karl Young at Wisconsin and Yale. Among my teachers his dialectical opposite, Irving Babbitt, then regarded as a disaffected iconoclast because he spoke for a very much older order, used to call this old-boy network the "Philological Syndicate." Philology, as it had been handed on to them from Germany, was based upon old-fashioned linguistics (mostly early dialects, historical grammar, and etymology), plus an archaistic transcription of literary history which made it sound daring to venture for any length beyond the Middle Ages. Its regressive outlook was confirmed by reducing the dynamics of creative imagination to the interplay of sources and influences—a reduction which Harold Bloom has been updating and injecting with parricidal motives. Its consummation would lie in the assemblage of needed editions, such as F. N. Robinson's Chaucer and Edwin Greenlaw's Spenser. Textual collation was hardly as rigorous as it has since become, but it could be situated against prolegomenal background and surrounded with assiduous footnotes.

Critics and scholars were inclined to stand apart from one another in those bygone days. The critic had little standing within the university; the writer, as such, none at all. The influential handbook for graduate studies by René Wellek and Austin Warren, *Theory of Literature* (1949), might well be looked back upon as a landmark of subsequent change. A programmatic final chapter, to be dropped in later revision because the program was being so effectually realized, had posed a sharply pointed speculation: what if Kittredge, on retiring in 1930, had been succeeded by T. S. Eliot? But that was almost what had taken place, give or take a few years. Actually, when Kittredge retired in 1936, his hegemony was already on the wane, and his department was opening up to more innovative viewpoints. Eliot was present in the flesh for no more than a single year (1932–

33); but as Charles Eliot Norton Professor of Poetry he had delivered the lectures that would be published as *The Use of Poetry and the Use of Criticism,* and with Theodore Spencer had introduced a course on his British contemporaries. Spencer, F. O. Matthiessen, Douglas Bush, Archibald MacLeish, Reuben Brower, W. J. Bate, and others responsive to evolving tastes and canonical readjustments—soon reinforced by the presence of Eliot's critical comrade-in-arms, I. A. Richards—played their parts in shifting Harvard's center of curricular gravity.

The transition was more dramatic at Yale, which had previously advanced its focus to a nearer point in literary history: a comfortable enclosure amid the clubbable personalities and collectible memorabilia of the eighteenth century. With the advent of Cleanth Brooks and Robert Penn Warren—who, in addition to their individual contributions, had together produced the movement's anthology—and of its committed historian, Professor Wellek, and with the advocacy of its resident theorist, W. K. Wimsatt, New Criticism was welcomed into the academic establishment. This put a seal upon the pioneering endeavors and guiding periodicals at Vanderbilt, Louisiana State, and Kenyon College, where John Crowe Ransom was fulfilling his evangelical mission. Meanwhile criticism in the lower case, yet still relatively new, was figuring more and more widely in the curriculum. Such developments went hand in hand, as we now recognize, with the assimilation of Modernism and the attempt to meet the special claims it made upon its readers. Anglo-American critics were moving, somewhat belatedly, from the "appreciative" to the "analytic," in the late William Empson's terms. Richards, in his British classroom, had raised psychological questions about the traditional "principles," and had conducted "practical" analyses, not only of poems but of his students' responses to them. Empson, his most brilliant student, through a series of subtle explications, demonstrated the dynamic role of ambiguities in the poetic process.

Now the concept of ambiguity, by strict definition, specifies a double—rather than a multiple or polysemous—meaning, and posits an equivocal yet definite alternative, not much less specific than its overt signification. It was ordinarily presumed that the writer himself, typically a Metaphysical Poet, pointed the way from his literal denotations toward their connotative associations. The notion of "close reading" presupposed the possibility of bringing the reader closer and closer to some well-defined object. *Understanding Poetry,* for Brooks and Warren as for Richards before them, implied that there were hazards of misunderstanding, obstacles or faults which could be pedagogically surmounted or corrected. Henry James, in one of the most poignantly personal of his *nouvelles,* had proposed a metaphor for the hiatus between an author and his reviewers, *The Figure in the Carpet.* Evidently it had been inspired by his repeated experience of being misunderstood, not to say unappreciated. Full appreciation of his work would not come until his centennial, nearly a generation after his death, when his unfathomed supersubtlety would meet its match among the newest critics. In the game of wits between his story's persona and its fictitious readers, they had altogether missed the protagonist's "little secret," his "inner meaning," his "finest fullest intention." This, however, lurks in such recondite hiding that we cannot really blame the misunderstanders.

We might be dissuaded even further from any mediating inquiry by the well-known neocritical essay of Wimsatt and Monroe Beardsley, "The Intentional Fallacy." "Fallacy" was not the most apposite word for the difficulty as they addressed it; "heresy" would have served fairer notice, since it indicates a lapse from dogma rather than a mistake in logic. Wimsatt and Beardsley were issuing a timely caveat against an unconsidered dependence on biographical data or historical circumstance as a substitute for critical evaluation. Critics, they justifiably warned, should be careful not to take an author's wish for his deed. Intention, they proceeded to maintain, is "neither available nor desirable as a standard for judging the success" of any given work. But this is to isolate the act of judgment from criteria that might have some relevant bearing upon it; and it would be just as shortsighted to dismiss the writer's sense of purpose— seldom unavailable and often expressly stated—as it might have been to accept his aspirations at face value. Goethe had outlined the normative procedure when he suggested that we ask ourselves first what the author had intended, then whether it was worth while, and finally—conclusively—whether or not he had succeeded in accomplishing it. And with Goethe himself there could be no doubt that the design was apparent, that the task was worthy of the endeavor, or that the imaginative *Dichtung* had been conditioned by the living *Wahrheit*.

Yet Goethe was so overwhelming a personality that, in conflating life and work, he set an extreme example. Recent criticism, with Roland Barthes, seems to have been moving toward the opposite extreme: the demise of the author. Although this reversal has the helpful consequence of drawing more attention toward the purview of the reader, it seems to be one of those Gallic exaggerations which provoke more noise than light. Even more hyperbolic, if not nihilistic, is the declaration of Jacques Derrida that "nothing exists outside of the text." Certainly, if that arresting overstatement were the literal truth, it would subsist in a solipsistic vacuum; I would not be writing this and you would not be reading it. However, we might agree upon the primacy of a text as our middle ground, and upon your apprehension of it as the best warrant for its existence. Such an agreement, a minimal presupposition for critical discourse, places the emphasis on the admittedly problematic relationship of text to reader—on interpretation, in an arguable word. It is here that we encounter a gathering trend of recoil, which was signalized some twenty years ago by the polemical essay of Susan Sontag, "Against Interpretation." Its angry protest flanked a disarming plea for unmediated esthetic experience, as against the intrusions and confusions of those officious would-be interpreters who tended to get in its way.

Miss Sontag ended on a note of high bravura: "In place of a hermeneutics we need an erotics of art." But, inasmuch as sex involves direct contact, while reading is perforce a matter of verbal codes and mental processes, her trope is misleading—unless she was advising us to read the *Kamasutra*. If we renounced interpreters, we would not put an end to interpretation; we would merely be interpreting for ourselves, and possibly missing a good deal for lack of training or information. Insofar as reality is registered in our minds, Nietzsche has observed, "facts do not exist, only interpretations." These relate us to others through language, to nature through science, to society through law, to the past through history. Aristotle's encyclopedic worldview had its logical starting point in his brief treatise on method, *De Interpretatione.* Hermeneutics, confronted with the hermetic mysteries of religion, devised varying approaches: scriptural, scholastic, talmudic, cabbalistic. Confronting a verifiable chain of induction, Champollion could decipher the hieroglyphics on the Rosetta Stone. Theorizing on natural selection, Darwin could arrive at a plausible explanation for the origin of species. Certain writers have told us how they want to be interpreted, Dante more explicitly than Goethe. In his explanatory letter to Can Grande della Scala, outlining the scheme of fourfold exegesis, he invited his reader to connive with him in the intentional fallacy. Joyce's main theme, after all, was a writer's intentions.

And yet, if Susan Sontag was crying in the wilderness, her remonstrance against interpretation has been gaining critical reinforcement. "The widespread and unquestioning notion that the critic's job is to interpret literary works" has become, for Jonathan Culler, an "insidious legacy." It is a waste, he believes, of energies that could be more profitably centered upon those "conditions of meaning" which have been too thoughtlessly glossed over or taken for granted. Speaking for a more conservative school of thought, more attentive to the authorial viewpoint, E. D. Hirsch too would call for a moratorium on interpretation. This, as I understand it, would not necessarily be a repudiation of the interpretative process or an invalidation of what we might have been learning through it. It could simply be an acknowledgment that, at the stage we have reached, accumulation has glutted the supply. A consensus has built up around each of our major writers, which—though by no means unanimous—voices a whole range of expectable views. To press beyond it is to strain for novelty. The latter-day interpreter is anticipated by received opinion at every step. Small wonder, if he seeks for "defamiliarization." The inherent, if redundant, tendency of pedagogic routine is to stick with it, repeat it, and pass it on. To "make it new," and still seem true, gets harder and harder; any innovation is more likely to seem an overreading, either half-baked or far-fetched.

If such a moratorium were declared, we could live more or less comfortably upon the existing wordhoard for at least another generation. It could be an open season for reviewing or digesting what had been expressed and overlooked. Teachers could carry on, as they truly must, by instilling the lore they had been taught. But if they were teaching at a university, they also had to demonstrate that they were scholars. The standard habilitation has been the Ph.D. thesis, which purported to be something more than a *specimen eruditionis,* conscientiously touching all the familiar bases. It was expected moreover to set forth a contribution to knowledge, breaking new ground in its field. That assumption has been overstrained by an increasing scale of operations and a decreasing level of prerequisites. It has been twenty years, again, since I had occasion to notice: "Learned journals multiply for the advancement, not of learning, but of assistant professors." Printing costs have likewise multiplied, inordinately during the past two decades. Yet the multiplication of periodicals and monographs has turned out to be more diffuse and repetitious than ever, though with less impact—perused by few except competing specialists or potential employers. The exhortation "publish or perish" has yielded an efflorescence of publications distinguished by their perishability. Careers, like that of Borges' Pierre Menard, have been spent in frustrated replication.

Literature is not subject to linear progress, as Marx himself allowed, when contrasting the Homeric epos with contemporary journalism. Criticism, as it accumulates, can move along and broaden its perspectives; yet it cannot be viewed as progressive in any scientific sense, since its latest findings need not displace the earlier ones. We could briefly illustrate from its greatest example. "About anyone so great as Shakespeare," wrote T. S. Eliot in 1927, "it is probable that we can never be right; and if we can never be right, it is better that we should from time to time change our way of being wrong." This seems to bespeak some uniquely distinctive configuration in Shakespeare's carpet, albeit one that is forever fated to remain inscrutable. But Eliot went on to argue a tentative case for the predominating influence of Senecanism. His immediate inspiration was a new edition of the Elizabethan Seneca. His ulterior motive was to show, by an invidious comparison between Stoicism and Thomism, that Shakespeare was philosophically inferior to Dante. As a matter of fact, the argument that Shakespeare was strongly influenced by Stoic throught and Senecan technique had been heavily implemented by the doctoral dissertation of J. W. Cunliffe in 1893. Philological scholarship then was deeply immersed in *Quellenforschung,* in accounting for masterpieces by digging up sources, and hence in tracing Shakespeare back to one or another of his numerous literary models.

Eliot has ceased to be—what he had become in his lifetime—an oracle, and even then Shakespearean research was ready to prove him wrong in a newer way. In 1934 Willard Farnham brought out *The Mediaeval Heritage of Elizabethan Tragedy,* a comprehensive study which minimized classical prototypes while stressing indigenous backgrounds. Anti-Senecanism was soon pushed farther—probably too far—by the dissertation of Howard Baker, *Induction to Tragedy* (1939), which mitigated its polemics with a sensitive chapter on the origins of blank verse. Now, as it happens, just the other day I saw the announcement for a forthcoming monograph which promises to renew our conception of Shakespeare by viewing him in the light of Senecan influence after all. The Stoic tragedian would not have been surprised at watching the wheel of Fortune come full circle. As for Shakespeare, like all of the greatest writers, he undoubtedly merits continual reinterpretation, not only because his work is so rich in nuances to be discerned through rereading, but also because each successive generation must formulate its own relations with him. This turnover is bound to leave an awkward clutter of duplication, wasted effort, planned obsolescence, and wrongheaded surmise. Shakespearean performance is affected by the same pressures; revivals seek to justify themselves by a deliberate alteration of characteristic features; and the director becomes an *auteur* who freely revises his playwright's original script.

The endless reconsideration of lesser writers may raise larger doubts. The very passage of time, which affords a chance for adjustment to changed conditions, has furthermore a winnowing effect. We no longer regard Carlyle as a serious thinker, or Meredith as an important novelist, even though they barely survive in a kind of antiquarian limbo. Once a body of works has been incorporated into a canon, enlargement comes more easily than exclusion—especially when scholars are looking for subjects. Some of us,who can still recall the ban on *Ulysses,* smuggled Joyce into the course-offering a few years afterwards, and have lived to witness his transfiguration into an academic industry. Melville has been all but drowned in a deluge of commentary, yet he died in utter obscurity and was virtually ignored for the next thirty years. Faulkner, largely through the accidents of translation, enjoyed the happier fate of recognition abroad in mid-career. Specialization has been developing so fast that we scarcely appreciate the irony of designating certain professors of English as Joyceans, Melvilleans, or Faulknerians, as if those were prestigious full-time jobs. It is understandable why their juniors, emerging from graduate school with claims to stake and reputations to make, should be intent upon canonizing less celebrated figures. A professorship in Thurber Studies, or so I am informed, has been endowed at one of our leading state universities.

We could react by reviving Sainte-Beuve's question, "What is a classic?" He was proposing to extend that rubric of critical acceptance from Ancients to Moderns, and—over a wider distance—from West to East. The corpus of great books, as inherited by the Humanists from the Greeks and Romans, had for many centuries formed the staple of education in the liberal arts. Those *auctores,* monuments and documents at once, were the authorities of classical culture. In a widening world they continued to stand for the shared memories of past civilization, but were gradually eroded as a viable frame of universal reference. They would be increasingly supplemented, and partially superseded, after the English classics were admitted to the canon. The rate of admission has been accelerated of late; in the quest for more authors to interpret, the probationary lag has been cut down between Grub Street and Mount Parnassus. While the Modernists were live contemporaries, the Academy was reluctant and slow to accept them. That was the usual observance, for they were professedly unacademic, and readers could relate to them more directly than to their dead predecessors, who required more in the way of classroom resurrection. Their present successors have, for the most part, reverted to simpler modalities. Yet younger academics seem overeager to publicize their unconsummated careers, and to organize them into a non-descript movement loosely identifiable as Post-Modernism.

With the recognition of American literature, theretofore neglected by English departments, a vast and fertile territory was opened for cultivation just two generations ago. The ensuing rush and energetic settlement—abetted by nationalistic expansiveness—have reaped harvests of artistic enrichment and cultural self-awareness. If Melville furnished the outstanding instance of vindicated neglect, there have been many others. But, in view of historical limitations, there could not have been many of his stature. After their attractions had been explored, the exploration shifted to minor writers, and all too frequently strove to convert modest geese into overvalued swans. Such inflations push the canon toward disintegration. Meanwhile an interpretative consensus has been so conformably established that Sacvan Bercovitch has recently been advocating a "dissensus." Canonical extension has also drawn upon such developing areas as Black Studies and Women's Studies. Here the limitation was the injustice of social conditions, which in the past had restricted the means of expression. Literacy itself had been so restricted among the blacks that, until latterly, published writings had to be looked upon as fortunate exceptions. Women, in undue subordination, had nonetheless shared in high culture. Whenever they managed to write, they were limited to the more intimate and less public genres: lyric and novel, rather than epic and drama. There they could do as well as, and sometimes better than, their masculine peers.

In both of those busy fields the rediscovery and revaluation of texts have been guided by sociological interests rather than by preexisting literary standards. This revisionism constitutes a critical equivalent for Affirmative Action. Its extraliterary criterion was laid down by ideology: Feminism derives its values from gender as Marxism does from class. In our era of transvaluations it is not surprising that Marxist criticism should be undergoing revival within non-Marxist countries, nor that—in the wake of Lukács, Benjamin, and the Frankfurt School—it should be taking more sophisticated stands. Those of us who witnessed the 1930s might recall *The Great Tradition* by Granville Hicks, wherein American writers were revaluated by the touchstones of a hypothetical proletariat. Shortly thereafter another book came out under the same title, wherein F. R. Leavis propounded his private party-line on English novelists. Thus two different canons appealed for support to tradition; equally doctrinaire, they subscribed to conflicting doctrines. An additional code of indoctrination, deriving from Freud, is not so much a revival as a fluctuating continuity. Psychoanalysis, as applied to literature through the *séminaires* of Jacques Lacan, sketches the freest fantasias on the most reductive themes. Both the Freudian and the Marxian methods, like the Black and the Feminist, substantially depend upon content analysis. None of them has shown much concern for the formal or cognitive aspects of writing.

Accordingly, if we are still in the habit of reading literature as a record of the human condition, their apperceptions might well change our minds or alert us to something that we had missed. They can present some fresh and fairly extensive grounds for reinterpretation. That, however, would appear to be work of supererogation, from the standpoint of Professor Culler, who is anxious "not to produce yet another interpretation . . . but to advance one's understanding of the conventions and operations of an institution, a mode of discourse." His preferred alternative, deconstruction, does not tell us very much about conventions or institutions, but focuses intensively upon the operations of discourse. The word itself, one of M. Derrida's profuse coinages, pointedly reverses the aim of reconstruction—of following a writer's conception, step by step, to its fulfillment—which has been a model for intentionalists (not excluding Empson). Like *analysis,* as opposed to *synthesis,* it suggests the critical function of taking things apart in order to see how they work. But the emphasis here seems to fall upon breaking them down, on dismantling and decomposition, while such habitual metaphors as unmasking, teasing, and tinkering *(bricolage)* do not hold much promise for putting them together again. Despite one ponderous title, *De la Grammatologie,* the systematic treatise is decidedly not M. Derrida's genre; for he is an inveterate reinterpreter, who spins off his points in discursive essays.

These take their departure from marginal—even tangential—comments upon a sequence of elusive texts, most of them interpretations themselves rather than more purely literary excerpts, which have been carefully chosen from such refractory masters as Nietzsche, Mallarmé, and Jean Genet. A strategic formulation, expounding through wordplay a passage from Rousseau's *Confessions,* equates the art of writing with the act of masturbation. This does not take us very far toward an erotics of art. Yet it serves as a metaphorical warning against expecting too much in the way of linguistic "intercourse" (Saussure borrowed that English noun, it should be remembered, to emphasize the social objectives of language). To read along with Derrida is to undermine our overconfidence in communing or intercommunication, in meeting other minds of getting our meanings across, in the mutuality of written expression. What the various Structuralists held in common was their substitution of correlations for entities. Starting there, the Post-Structuralists have moved on to cut off the correlations. The inevitable difference between whatever writers may say and what it might mean to others was the premise for Paul de Man's paradoxical inference: that critics showed more insight when they were blind to their own presumptions. But who, in that sightless kingdom, could pronounce that one-eyed judgment, if not another critic? For de Man a text was less valid than its extrapolated subtext; and therefore, reversing Coleridge, allegory was privileged over symbolism.

A misreading, for Richards, had been an aberration; for Professor Bloom it could be sheer serendipity. The question that arises with M. Derrida is whether there can be anything but misreading—and thence, its corollary, whether there could be any such thing as a misreading. If everything is misreading, then nothing is. It should be acknowledged that to accompany him on his commentator's forays can be a suggestive and fascinating excursion. Though he comes down rigorously upon the prose of others, his own style remains playful, almost capricious, confessedly "exorbitant" at times, perhaps because of a basic skepticism about the use of words. Logical demonstration gives way to free association, characteristically clinched by a *jeu de mots,* such as the pun that links "difference" with "deferral" *(différance).* Each analytic exercise is taken up as a challenge to reveal internal contradictions, though it never terminates in a resolution. If there is any end in sight, it is an impasse *(aporía)* or stoppage *(epoché)* or otherwise, in more scribal terms, a bracketing or erasure. On a more philosophical plane of abstraction, it is *Aufhebung* or suspension, and it bears the imprint of Derrida's mentor, Heidegger, the most logocentric of modern metaphysicians. Facing the gap or gulf that has been so meticulously pointed out, standing at the brink of that stylistic abyss, we are well advised to pause and reflect. But should that stop—that *mise en abîme*—become our destination?

Now we have much to learn from those who admonish us not to be too simplistic, interposing objections and indicating disparities. Whatever we are trying to analyze is more complicated than we might have thought, more often than not, and physics would have stagnated by assuming that the atom was the ultimate particle. Yet the rationale of stopping at a checkpoint, after duly checking, is to proceed on one's course. If a textual editor runs into a crux or a garbling, he tries to make sense of it through conjectural emendation. Philosophers do not withdraw from further speculation, nor scientists from continuing research, after having enunciated the principles of undecidability or indeterminacy. Why should critics be consigned to spending the rest of their lives in an intellectual quarantine of dangling signifiers and impounded uncertainties? Pondering Derrida's arguments, George Steiner has emphatically conceded that for "deconstructive semiotics" he can see no "logical or epistemological refutation." Instead, the sole mode of escape from its dilemmas that he would recommend is theological in its implications: "transcendence," "moral intuition," "act of faith." Not that criticism has to be grounded in religion, but that it is left to depend upon make-believe: "We must read *as if . . .*" (It may be historically ironic that Professor Steiner's lecture was presented in a series named for Leslie Stephen, the rationalistic interpreter of the Enlightenment.)

Should we be put off by so probing a critique of textuality? Need we be so easily intimidated by such forebodings of epistemological stalemate? "As a philospher," Simone de Beauvoir once remarked to Arthur Koestler (and was overheard by Stephen Spender), "you must realize that each of us, when he looks at a *morceau de sucre,* sees an entirely different object." This is true enough to be obvious; yet neither would have had any trouble in recognizing, discussing, or consuming a lump of sugar. Philosophy would have bogged down at its outset, if it had no resources for progressing beyond the elementary quandaries of subjectivity. Trained as a philosopher, Jacques Derrida can be adept at salutary caveats and heuristic propositions. He is more in his element when he plays the gadfly than when he is hallowed as a guru. His ascendancy, on the other hand, seems to be attested mainly by students and teachers of literature, more in the habit of adducing than of questioning authority; and his questions tend to become their answers. Without much philosophical orientation of their own, they seem better versed in parroting phrases, bandying terms, and dropping names than in cogent reasoning. Much of their jargon seems to re-echo, at a third remove, the metaphysical verbalism of the German Phenomenologists. In the long run they may discover that their studies in language converge more naturally, and more empirically, with the Linguistic and Analytic Philosophers of the Anglo-American school.

Blocked at one side of a bilateral area, wherein oppositions thrive and binary choices are acted out, we can still search for an opening in the other direction. Deconstructionism, as a theory of knowledge, may prove quite as unyielding and absolute as Professor Steiner has insisted, and we might not be able to overcome that Sisyphean resistance which it seems to stimulate. If we are thereby tempted to back down and give up, resigning ourselves to a prospect of perpetual absence and unbreakable silence, then we have no ontological warrant for engaging further in criticism—or, indeed, in much else. Why should we go on undertaking to read the unreadable? "Whereof one cannot speak, thereof one must be silent," as Wittgenstein concluded in his *Tractatus Logico-Philosophicus*. But that was not the last word; he persisted at length and in depth with his *Philosophical Investigations*—rather more articulately than those Post-Structuralist critics who, having bypassed Derrida's hard version of deconstruction, seem to be opting for a soft one. Their path has been cleared by dropping out the incidentals of history and of authorship. To the critical query, "What does this text mean?," Tzvetan Todorov has not uncritically responded that there could now be two contradictory answers. The first would be a tough-minded rejection: "Nothing." But, once the routines had been suspended, the second answer could be softened into a tender-minded complicity: "Anything."

Thus theoretical arguments can be reduced to trendy shib-boleths, which in turn can operate as signals to announce that anything could go: here is a fresh start which might lead almost anywhere, a new game which improvises its rules as it goes along. It must exert a particular attraction for graduate students and younger teachers, who may well feel constrained by the cumulative weight of the academic backlog preceding them. They have been conceptually licensed by this sweeping gesture of release to glide past the methodological impedimenta of bio-graphies, periods, and genres. Though they are preoccupied with texts in the abstract, they seem much less interested in citing, quoting, comparing, or explicating concrete examples. Many of these emergent desconstructionists seem to be more conversant with the latest theories than well-read in the tradi-tional body of writing that comprises literature. Yet there can be little doubt but that they have succeeded in reopening a floodgate, or that our literary lowlands will soon be inundated by the rising tides of wayward reinterpretation. "Every decoding is another encoding." That pithy axiom, whether it be construed as a frustration or an incitement, is more than a reaffirmation of hermeneutic circularity. As exemplified by David Lodge in his fictional parody, *Small World,* it is shown to be a political platform for a bustling international network of slogans, pub-lications, conferences, and professorial chairs.

Doubtless critics should have ample opportunity to generate rereadings, reconsider questions endlessly moot, and rewrite the palimpsests of previous generations. Under an unbridled dis-pensation, it should be easier for them to display originality, albeit at the possible expense of solidity, conviction, or dis-cernment. For, the farther out they go, the less feasible it will become to verify or authenticate their opinions. If we are con-cerned with verification, we must consider not only the inter-preter but also what might be termed the interpretee, the reader who must be convinced, for whom the critic tries to make the text more meaningful. And if we are concerned with authen-ticity, we must pay due attention to what has been signified, to the referent in the situation at hand. Literary artifacts, being composed of words, cannot cast off the trammels of their intrinsic literariness. Nonetheless we can take account of those self-conscious habits without retreating to the tenuous sophistry that literature deals with nothing but itself. That is precisely what our archetypal novel, *Don Quixote,* is all about. To mistake windmills for giants is to be deluded, of course; but to puncture the illusion is to clarify our perception, to distinguish fantasy from actuality. Representations can never measure up to realities, and it would be naive to confound the two categories. Yet this is not to deny that reality exists, nor to preclude us from seeking its imperfect adumbration through books.

The art of fiction, as an intended imitation of life, is mimetic to a greater or lesser degree. But mimicry is not identity; it can never be as realistic as novelists have always liked to pretend; at the most it is a symbolic approximation rather than a literal reproduction. As the most popular of literary forms, it could convey a widespread collective impression, so that—much as we might disagree about certain fictitious characters—we lend them the status of human beings whenever we talk about them. We no longer talk very much about taste—*de gustibus non disputandum*—since its hierarchical standards have lost their authority under our heterogeneous culture. And though we still appeal to common sense now and then, usually when we are rejecting idiosyncrasy, the phrase itself no longer denotes an established community of ideas *(sensus communis)* or resounds with a Johnsonian evocation of cultural norms. Its antithesis, nonsense, was so designated by the Age of Reason: "True No-meaning," declared Alexander Pope, "puzzles more than Wit." Living in what the Existentialists have dramatized as the Age of Absurdity, it is true meaning that puzzles us. Called upon to mourn the death of the novel, along with the death of the author, we may wonder how such obsequies reflect upon the living writers of this Post-Modernist era. It is no wonder that, as criteria lapse, critics lose their bearings.

If they seem to be wandering in a wilderness, Geoffrey Hartman would redeem that trope by envisioning a promised land, plus the tablets of a renovated law. Tzvetan Todorov would be less sanguine about the current state-of-the art, yet would look ahead with "a hermeneutic optimism." His *Critique de la Critique* may reverberate, in American ears, with a distant echo of H. L. Mencken's "Criticism of Criticism of Criticism." By that titular echolalia Mencken sought to deprecate his subject-matter as derivative, attenuating, and parasitical. He was rebutting proposals from J. E. Springarn and others for a "creative criticism"—which have their counterpart today in the unabashed presumption that the critic somehow transcends whatever he condescends to criticize, that art exists for criticism's sake. Since English uses two words where French must rely on a *double-entendre,* M. Todorov's title should be rendered as *A Critique of Criticism.* One of the most resourceful and knowledgeable among the literary Structuralists, he has refused to fall in with his self-appointed successors among the Post-Structuralists. The colleagues whom he now singles out for approval, Paul Bénichou (*Morales du Grand Siècle,* studies in French Romanticism) and Ian Watt (*The Rise of the Novel,* a critical biography of Conrad), though they are admirable literary historians, remain unreconstructed Pre-Structuralists.

History can never be avoided for long, though the attitudes and techniques of its reinterpreters have been continually modified by historic vicissitude. Some periods have been more acutely conscious of this than others, conspicuously the Elizabethan epoch; such recent studies as those of Stephen Greenblatt, however selectively and subjectively, have been documenting that rapprochement. Conversely, historicism could have been ignored during the centuries when Virgil's *Fourth Eclogue* was interpreted by scholiasts as a prophecy announcing the birth of Christ—and that creative misinterpretation enjoyed a curious history of its own. The most flagrant misinterpreters of Shakespeare happened to be two other major writers, both of them to some extent historians, each of them motivated by a personal animosity. Voltaire censured Shakespeare unhistorically, as a rival whose plays offended the neoclassical rules. Tolstoy held an anti-Shakespearean bias, as George Orwell has argued, which prefigured the Lear-like tragedy that he was preparing for himself. It would take an unbiased critical insight to penetrate the psychology of that authorial blindness. Lives and works are not wholly interdependent, but we risk misconception by disre-

garding the clues that biography might turn up. Dr. Johnson
made his authoritative approach through *Lives of the Poets*. If
his criticism is better remembered than his other writing, iron-
ically, he is best remembered as a biographical figure.

Obviously, the role of the author has not been, and will not
be, successfully eliminated (in Johnson's case it seems to have
been the text that went into abeyance). Biographical interpretation seems to be flourishing more strongly than ever among
a majority of our contemporaries—if we may judge by noting
that it has enlisted the principal efforts of such accomplished
scholar-critics as Leon Edel (on James), Richard Ellmann (on
Joyce), Joseph Frank (on Dostoevsky), W. J. Bate (on Keats
and Johnson), and Cynthia Wolff (on Edith Wharton and Emily
Dickinson). To be sure, the wider public interest in these works
centers upon personalities and careers. However, they can lead
us back to the sphere of artistic individuality, to an awareness
of the writer as an artificer putting his signature on his crafts-
manship, and to the initiatives of the literary creator in deter-
mining the nature of his creations. This may seem a reversion
to an outdated and lapsed priority; but it has been renewed and
reinforced by the importance that Mikhail Bakhtin accorded to
"the act of authorship." The recovery and translation of Bakhtin's many contributions, which range from Marx to Freud and
from Dostoevsky to Rabelais, bring home to us how much the
uniqueness of individual authors has enriched the diversity of
literature as a whole. Nor is the reader left out; for human
utterance, as Bakhtin conceived it, is never a monologue; it
embraces all parties to it in a dialogic interaction.

Readerly and writerly concerns, though differently oriented
and ordered, are clearly corresponsive to such a dialogue. Neither could be meaningfully excluded, nor could either dispense
with the other. But, at a time when paradigms are shifting, it
is not unusual to promote the controversial innovations by
downgrading the accepted constituents. The critical enterprise
should be pluralistic enough to retain its stability while undergoing renewal. Theory does not encroach upon practice, as some
have worried; neither does it justify itself unless practice bears
out its conceptual schemes. To study the conditions of meaning
is, as it were, to interpret interpretation. And semiotic theory

has much to teach the practical interpreter, who could profit from more analytic approaches to the vocabulary of signs and the repertory of codes. Classical rhetoric, comparative literature, theories and methods of old and New Criticism have already contributed an assortment of tools. Even philology had its taxonomies, its rudimentary systems of classification, plus its commitment to etiology, to textual origins and historical backgrounds. There has been a concentration since upon morphology—if we may so describe the stress on form, on stylistics, genres, and technical devices. Those who would move on from there are postulating a physiology of literature, an organic and functional investigation of its workings, in conjunction with linguistics, psychology, philosophy, and other cross-fertilizing disciplines.

T. S. Eliot's only piece of advice for aspiring critics was to be as intelligent as possible—which may have been adequate for Eliot himself, but would not offer much guidance to the less gifted, to the rest of us. Since reading cannot but be an educational process at every level, from learning one's letters to reviewing *The Waste Land,* normally the critic recapitulates a progression from student to teacher. After he has gained his expertise, he can impart it to his pupil, the general reader, who may still be striving toward that qualified level of reading skill which Professor Culler would accredit as competence. If we seek a didactic model, we can find one where there are so many, in *The Pilgrim's Progress.* The Everyman of Bunyan's parable, at the beginning of his pilgrimage through the ups and downs of life, stops for a preparatory briefing at the Interpreter's House. This is a kind of allegorical sideshow, whose presiding master expounds its scriptural and proverbial object-lessons: "things rare and profitable." The traveler, though he looks and listens earnestly and patiently, seems more and more eager to be on his way toward the luminous goal. It is an arduous journey; but, fortified by all that he has learned along the way, he will attain his great reward. He will become an interpreter in his own right; he will be able to read the experience for himself; he will confront the final text face to face; and its meaning will be his interpretation.

NATHAN A. SCOTT, JR.

On the Teaching of Literature
in an Age of Carnival

Undergraduates electing programs of concentration in English studies toward the end of preparing for graduate work in
the field and for academic careers are, I suspect, by no means
so numerous today as they were, say, in the 1950s; but the best
among them are, in my experience, as able and as serious as
were the best of their predecessors a generation ago. And for
them the charm of the modern canon in literature is no less
tyrannous than it was in the student community of that earlier
time. True, their "theologians" are no longer Cleanth Brooks
and Lionel Trilling and Northrop Frye, but rather such people
as Jacques Derrida and Harold Bloom and Stanley Fish; yet
their "sacred texts" are still drawn from the writings of such
poets as Rilke and Eliot and Stevens and Lowell and such novelists and dramatists as Mann, Joyce, Kafka, Brecht, Faulkner,
and Beckett. Which is to say that literature is their religion.

Indeed, it is out of just the kind of immense moral and spiritual authority the young are inclined to impute to the literature
that fascinates them that there arises what may well be the most
difficult pedagogical issue presented by the college literary classroom. For the best and the brightest of one's students tend to
be so much like young Charles Dilke. Here, the scene that I
have in mind is a certain evening in late December of 1817,

when John Keats was walking back from London to Hampstead
in the company of his good friends and Hampstead neighbors
Charles Armitage Brown and Charles Wentworth Dilke, the
three having been to London for the Boxing Day opening of a
pantomime in the Drury Lane theatre. Brown was a young
Scotsman with strong literary interests who owned a house ad-
joining Dilke's on the edge of Hampstead Heath. And Dilke
himself, though at the time holding a post in the Navy Pay
Office, was already launching what was to become a long and
successful career as essayist and editor. Among these three there
was much warmly affectionate liking, and, on this particular
night, they were having (as Keats later reported in a letter to
his brothers George and Tom) "not a dispute but a disquisition."
Dilke was a man who, as Keats later said, could not even "feel
he [had] . . . a personal identity unless he [had] . . . made up
his Mind about every thing": he was one "incapable of remaining
content with half knowledge"—which prompted Keats to suspect that he might "never come at a truth as long as he lives;
because he is always trying at it."[1] So, as the three young men
thrashed out whatever it was they were ventilating, Dilke was
very probably laying about in his customary manner, being confident of the genial tolerance of his friends. And, said Keats,
as their "disquisition" proceeded, "several things dovetailed in
my mind, & at once it struck me, what quality went to form a
Man of Achievement especially in Literature . . . I mean *Negative Capability,* that is when man is capable of being in uncertainties, Mysteries, doubts, without any irritable reaching after
fact & reason."[2]

Now the atmosphere of the undergraduate classroom is influenced perhaps by nothing so much as by the fact that the
most articulate and talented of the young people who are there
for instruction tend very often, in their eagerness for enlargement of mind and spirit, to lack any capacity for tolerance of
the ambiguous and the uncertain, and, like Keats's friend Dilke,
their impatience with what is dark and fugitive makes reflection

1. *The Letters of John Keats,* 2 vols, ed. Hyder Edward Rollins (Cambridge,
Mass.: Harvard University Press, 1958), II, p. 213.
2. *Letters of Keats,* I, p. 193.

for them a kind of "straining at a moveless latch." Or, one might say that they approach *Heart of Darkness* or *Little Gidding* or Beckett's *Godot* as though they were a clenched fist, as though the mysteries over which these texts hover could simply be battered open. It is not that they are unresponsive to the various complex considerations of form and literary craft with which strenuous reading must deal: on the contrary, these are matters in which they generally take an ardent interest. But challenging as they find questions of genre, metrics, prose conventions, and so on, their inclination is to regard such questions as at last ancillary to the doctrinal intentions of Yeats and Lawrence and Stevens and Bellow—and they do not intend to be too much put off by penultimate issues, for the fierce energy of mind that they descry in *The Tower* and *Women in Love* and *Transport to Summer* and *Herzog* prompts in them a sense of the necessity of quickly responding in terms either of approbation or dissent. So they rush toward a kind of forensic entanglement with the text at hand, and do so with such determination that one wonders (to rephrase Keats) if they will ever come at the sorts of insights literary experience may afford, so pertinaciously are they trying at them.

The ghost of Matthew Arnold will not, of course, at first be thought to have any sort of continuing life amongst the young in our period, but one has only to remark the reverential hush that settles down over a large campus auditorium at the moment before some distinguished visiting poet or critic is to speak, a hush that suddenly makes the occasion something like a Methodist prayer meeting—one has only to remark the fervent expectancy of this solemn raptus to know that the literary young are indeed as much persuaded as was Arnold that we must "turn to poetry to interpret life for us, to console us, to sustain us."[3] And when literature is depended upon for such guidance and solace, it will naturally be felt to be (as Arnold would say) "of the highest importance" that the wheat be separated from the chaff: so, in the manner of a Dilke, one will want soon to have "made up his mind" about the cogency, or lack of it, with which

3. Matthew Arnold, "The Study of Poetry," in *Essays in Criticism,* Second Series (London: Macmillan, 1896), p. 2.

a given text delivers its version of the human story, and that virtue which Keats considered to be essential to any serious literary venture—namely, Negative Capability, the capacity for tolerance of the ambiguous and the problematical—will prove to be very difficult of attainment.

And thus it would seem that, before and after all lessons regarding critical strategy have been laid down, the teaching enterprise needs to commit itself to what is perhaps the most basic hermeneutical effort to be undertaken in the classroom, of shutting off that anxious, peremptory talkativeness which presumes prematurely to handle literature in judicial ways. Such an effort must be undertaken not only for the sake of giving one's students a chance at the full literary experience, but also for the sake of preparing them to dwell in what is, as we might say following Mikhail Bakhtin, an age of carnival. The concept of carnival is, of course, an essential element of Bakhtin's theory of literature, for he considers the novel—which is for him the genre above all others—to be saturated with the carnival spirit.[4] I do not want, however, on this present occasion, to attempt any review of his highly complex argument about the role the carnivalesque plays in fiction: I want, rather, only to recall his conception of carnival as such, in its purest ideality. And, in this connection, the first thing to be said is that, for him, a time of carnival is one in which "life [is] drawn out of its *usual* rut" or is in some radical way " 'turned inside out.' "[5] That is to say, all the customary hierarchical structures and all the conventional norms and protocols are suspended, as the common life is invaded by a great wave of riotous antinomianism which makes everywhere for bizarre *mésalliances*. Things that are normally separate and distinct are brought together, so that "the sacred [combines] with the profane, the lofty with the low, the great with the insignificant, the wise with the stupid."[6] And the presiding spirit of blasphemy finds its quintessential expression in

4. *See* Mikhail Bakhtin, *Problems of Dostoevsky's Poetics*, ed. and trans. Caryl Emerson (Minneapolis: University of Minnesota Press, 1984), pp. 101–180; and also his *Rabelais and His World*, trans. Hélène Iswolsky (Cambridge, Mass.: MIT Press, 1968), *passim*.

5. *Problems of Dostoevsky's Poetics*, p. 122.

6. *Problems of Dostoevsky's Poetics*, p. 123.

the ritual of the mock crowning and subsequent decrowning of the carnival king—who is the very antithesis of a real king, since he is often in fact a slave or a jester. In short, everything is topsy-turvy, and the disarray thus engenders an uproarious kind of laughter. But the laughter belonging to carnival is no more the laughter of absolute negation than it is the laughter of absolute affirmation, for what Bakhtin takes to be the most fundamental fact about carnival is that, under its strange kind of dispensation, ambivalence of viewpoint is the prevailing sentiment: *nothing* is accorded a privileged status, and *everything* is relativized.

So in Bakhtin's sense of the term, ours seems now to be an age of carnival, for the myriad disjunctions that fracture and disunite cultural discourse in our period make all our forums a scene of Babel. What is clear beyond question is the extreme unlikelihood that the people of the West shall ever again be presented with any great, overarching *speculum mentis* that subdues all the entanglements of modern intellectual life and integrates the various fields of culture, assigning to each its proper place within the terms of some magnificently comprehensive map of the human universe. Nothing, indeed, could be more phantasmal, for the name of the game that we are fated to play (the game that organizes *our* culture and *our* consciousness) is pluralism. Which means that, instead of irritably reaching after what Keats calls "fact and reason," we must seek to win that special virtue which will enable us equally to dwell amidst the ambiguity and contrariety—and the irreversible relativism— that define our own late stage of modernity. And thus a literary education adequate to such a necessity will be one guided by a kind of pedagogy that, in fostering a proper reticence in students about *prematurely* engaging in "close bargaining" with literary representations, does in some measure prepare them to cope with the larger world beyond the classroom where, amidst the pervasive cultural fragmentation of the age, they will find themselves summoned to an ethos of encounter and required to reckon, without recourse to any sort of reductionism, with the multitudinous messages and voices that press in upon them, each clamoring for attention and for pride of place.

In such a world the real essence of "false consciousness" will be disclosed in anyone's effort at bullying others into some unilateral position which is declared to be foundational in respect to the rest of culture and therefore capable of adjudicating the claims of all other points of view. Choking off in this way what Michael Oakeshott calls "the conversation of mankind"[7] will doubtless be a recurrent temptation. Amidst all the exactions entailed in a cultural situation which is radically pluralistic, we are likely over and again to be assailed by the impulse impatiently to obliterate "dialogue" (as Bakhtin would say) by some form of "monologue." And a further temptation will be presented by some program of opposition to monologism which is but calculated to reinstate still another absolutism, as in the case of the currently seductive program of deconstruction.

The great lesson, of course, that Jacques Derrida wants to lay down is that language is without any foundation outside itself in which the play of language may be grounded, since anything that is accessible to the mind is itself "always already" organized by some system of signs and is thus merely another language. There is, in other words, absolutely nothing outside language itself, nothing which is immediately present to us as something which is elemental and self-confirming, as something in which language may find its "center" and with reference to which the determinate meaning of a given utterance may be established. Language in short, as the deconstructionists say, is not "motivated" ontologically by anything beyond itself: so, as the familiar figure of the late Paul de Man puts it, there is a certain "blindness" that is ineradicably a part of all discourse, since, however carefully supervised language may be, it can, in the final analysis, do nothing other than dramatize its own self-reflexiveness.

Now what kind of *Gesprächspartner* might we expect a good deconstructionist to be? Jürgen Habermas suggests, and I think rightly, that there can be no true dialogue apart from an ethos of generous democracy which rules out any element of "force" or "domination": the participants must, in other words, in some

---

7. *See* Michael Oakeshott, *The Voice of Poetry in the Conversation of Mankind* (London: Bowes and Bowes, 1959).

real sense accord one another the status of equality.[8] But, of course, for all its animosity toward "logocentrism," the very nature of the deconstructionist project militates against its according equality to any other cultural project. It is simply a matter of fundamental method: the deconstructionist is not, in Wordsworth's phrase, "a man speaking to men," but, rather, one who sets out to construe only for the sake of deconstruing. From Schleiermacher to Gadamer and from Dilthey to Ricoeur the tradition of hermeneutical reflection is to be found reminding us over and again that the process of understanding does perforce involve dialogue with whomever or whatever we are seeking to comprehend. True dialogue will doubtless involve interrogation and dispute, but the essential integrity of whoever or whatever is in front of us will not be initially contested, for such a procedure would cut the vital nerve of the dialogical possibility itself at the very outset. Yet this is precisely the procedure of deconstruction. It wants from the very beginning to dismantle, to root up, to eliminate, to erase: it intends to demonstrate that whatever it confronts is at cross-purposes with itself. Which means that, within the intellectual forum, deconstruction considers dialogue to be an antique sort of undertaking. "The point here is," as one commentator has said, "that you can't enter into a discussion with someone or something that has got you under analysis, and this is where deconstruction has always got you," for it puts you into the "position of not having a say, or not being able to answer back."[9] And thus, as it seems to me, Jacques Derrida and his various epigones are not to be counted on for any good guidance, as we cast about for a hermeneutical orientation of the literary classroom that may enable it more helpfully to prepare students to reckon with the challenge and the opportunity that are presented by the radically polyglot culture in which we find ourselves.

8. Jürgen Habermas, "The Hermeneutic Claim to Universality" ("Der Universalitätsanspruch der Hermeneutik," in his *Kultur and Kritik* [Frankfurt: Suhrkamp, 1973]), trans. Joseph Bleicher, and included in his *Contemporary Hermeneutics: Hermeneutics as Method, Philosophy and Critique* (London: Routledge and Kegan Paul, 1980), pp. 204–206.

9. Gerald L. Bruns, "Structuralism, Deconstruction, and Hermeneutics," *Diacritics*, 14, no. 1 (Spring 1984), p. 14.

To speak, however, of the pluralistic character of our culture as polyglot may not be altogether appropriate, since in this context the notion of the polyglot may seem to reinforce what is, I think, a mistaken view: namely, the presumption—fostered no doubt in part by Wittgenstein's posthumous influence—that the multiplicity of theory and doctrine and belief that we face in our time represents a great swarm of "language games" each of which, in being closed off from all others, is a kind of "windowless monad." But, as Habermas reminds us, "We are never locked within a single grammar. Rather, the first grammar that we learn to master already puts us in a position to step out of it and to interpret what is foreign, to make comprehensible what is incomprehensible, to assimilate in our own words what at first escapes them."[10] And thus the relativism entailed in a pluralistically ordered culture may not be so absolute as we are at first inclined to suppose.

Which is what we will also be reminded of by one of the crucial ideas of the great Russian literary theorist Mikhail Bakhtin. In his book on Dostoevsky and in the four long essays making up *The Dialogic Imagination,* Bakhtin develops a kind of speech-act theory that, despite its essential uniqueness, may be felt by English-speaking readers to bear certain resemblances to the thought of the Oxford philosopher, the late J. L. Austin. His guiding assumption is that the human order, in its most fundamental character, is dialogical and (as he says) "polyphonic." And this is why he regards the novel as the genre above all others, because he takes it to render a more adequate kind of justice to the polyphonic nature of human life than any other literary form. He consistently holds to a social conception of selfhood (not unlike that of the American thinker George Herbert Mead) and thus he considers the essential reality of the individual to be resident not in the detached, solitary ego but in the whole matrix of relations by which every person is formed. I am, for example, the result of a *paideia* administered by family, by Church, by certain educational institutions, by class, by na-

10. Jürgen Habermas, "A Review of Gadamer's *Truth and Method,*" in *Understanding and Social Inquiry,* ed. Fred Dallmayr and Thomas McCarthy (Notre Dame: University of Notre Dame Press, 1977), pp. 335–336.

tion, and countless other agencies. And the language I employ in spoken and written utterance is one that contrapuntally adjusts to one another all the voices emergent from these various places of my origin. My language, in other words, is not really mine, for one does "not, after all, [get one's language] out of a dictionary": "it exists in other people's mouths, in other people's contexts, serving other people's intentions: it is from there that one must take the word, and make it one's own."[11] Indeed, says Bakhtin, "The word in language is half someone else's."[12] So no speech act, whether spoken or written, can be claimed to be wholly original, for the world that we hold in common comprises many voices and many languages. The term that Bakhtin coined for this plurality is "heteroglossia"; his term for the dispersion and interpenetration in cultural discourse of our various language-games is "dialogized heteroglossia," which is the condition in which "concrete discourse finds the object at which it . . . [is] directed already . . . charged with value," since it is "shot though with . . . [other] thoughts . . . [and] points of view." Human life, in short, is a great polyphony of languages and voices which are constantly impinging upon and permeating one another in "a dialogically agitated . . . environment."[13] And the stance of the monologist, in its servitude to merely one language, is for Bakhtin the very type and example of *in*authenticity.

Michael Holquist, Bakhtin's ablest interpreter on the American scene, suggests that his entire project of building a dialogical theory of literature and rhetoric may be regarded as an extended "phenomenological meditation" on that great word of Christ's in the Sermon on the Mount: "All things . . . whatsoever ye would that men should do unto you, even so do ye also unto them" (Matthew 7: 12).[14] Here, as Professor Holquist

11. Mikhail Bakhtin, *The Dialogic Imagination,* ed. Michael Holquist and trans. Caryl Emerson and M. Holquist (Austin: University of Texas Press, 1981), p. 294.

12. *The Dialogic Imagination,* p. 293.

13. *The Dialogic Imagination,* p. 276.

14. Michael Holquist, "The Politics of Representation," in *Allegory and Representation,* ed. Stephen J. Greenblatt (Baltimore: The Johns Hopkins University Press, 1981), pp. 171–172.

feels, is the ethic that Bakhtin takes to be the controlling principle of cultural exchange, when it is truly responsive to the
essential logic of dialogue. But where does one turn for a hermeneutic that will keep us on such a high road—at once in
"Eng. 221" as well as in the complex relations of the public
order?

Certainly, as I have already suggested, one will not turn to
the deconstructionists, the New Inquisitors who receive their
instructions from Paris. But Bakhtin himself, I would propose,
will make a good point of departure. And then in which other
directions might we also be turning?

The remarkable sensitiveness with which Paul Ricoeur has
addressed himself to the entire range of issues in the field of
hermeneutical theory will surely at once put us in mind of him.
And his special relevance to an age of carnival, to a time of
radical pluralism, stems, I believe, precisely from the clarity
with which he perceives that ours is a period ineluctably marked
by "conflict of interpretations."[15] Nor is the elaborate program
that Ricoeur has developed in any way calculated to obliterate
this "conflict" by "totalizing" the multiplicity of interpretations
toward the end of some kind of "absolute synthesis." Indeed,
from his standpoint nothing could be more delusive than the
dream of such a synthesis, since he considers the pluralistic
character of our situation to be not merely a result of the cultural
exigencies belonging to late modernity but, more fundamentally, a result of the essential "finitude of [human] reflection"[16]
or of what he speaks of as "the perspectival limitation of perception" that "causes every view . . . to be a *point of view.*"
And this partiality of perspective that contaminates the entire
enterprise of thought is irremediable, because it is rooted in our
finitude, which may not itself simply be transcended. So any
kind of "absolute knowledge is impossible."[17] All "totalistic"
schemes, in other words, deserve to be distrusted, and thus, far

15. *See* Paul Ricoeur, *The Conflict of Interpretations: Essays in Hermeneutics,*
ed. Don Ihde and trans. by several hands (Evanston: Northwestern University
Press, 1974).

16. Paul Ricoeur, *Freud and Philosophy: An Essay on Interpretation,* trans.
Denis Savage (New Haven: Yale University Press, 1970), p. 379.

17. Ricoeur, *Freud and Philosophy,* p. 527.

from wanting to dissolve or annul the "heteroglossia" in which we find ourselves, Ricoeur's great purpose has been that of making manifest "the modalities . . . of interanimation between [the various] modes of discourse"[18] that give our culture its distinctive buzz and hum. As he says, "When Odysseus completes the circle and returns to his island of Ithaca there is slaughter and destruction. For me the philosophical task is not to close the circle, [or] to centralize or totalize knowledge, but to keep open the irreducible plurality of discourse"; and he reminds us that in order "to show how the different discourses may interrelate or intersect . . . one must resist the temptation to make them identical"[19] or to fashion some sort of monistic system whereby they may be hierarchically ordered and dominated. Which is to say that the only way of reckoning with a situation of radical pluralism in cultural life is to accept it and live *through* it, since it is only by way of such a "detour" that fundamental meanings and values in any field of inquiry are to be "retrieved."

We encounter a similar orientation in Hans-Georg Gadamer, a thinker who, perhaps beyond all others, deserves to be called the master strategist in the modern period of dialogical approaches to the hermeneutical problem; and his great book, *Truth and Method,* is today an unignorable text. His work is, of course, by no means without its problematic elements. He is, for one thing, more than a little touched by the cultural insularity so characteristic of German scholarship that has allowed him to neglect large ranges of Anglo-American thought from which, given the nature of his project, he might have been expected to take profit. And on other grounds his theoretical studies have been vigorously questioned by Jürgen Habermas, Emilio Betti, Wolfhart Pannenberg, E. D. Hirsch, and various others. But the heart of his program retains a powerful appeal. And perhaps his most fundamental proposal is simply that the event of understanding is one in which, forswearing any inten-

18. Paul Ricoeur, *The Rule of Metaphor,* trans. Robert Czerny et al. (Toronto: University of Toronto Press, 1977), p. 258.

19. "Dialogues with Paul Ricoeur," in Richard Kearney, *Dialogues with Contemporary Continental Thinkers* (Manchester: Manchester University Press, 1984), p. 27.

tion of seeking to control or manipulate that which is to be comprehended, we undertake instead to be utterly open to what it wants to say to us. Though his magnum opus, to be sure, is entitled *Truth and Method,* Gadamer's thought (as David Linge reminds us) is distinguished not so much by any new hermeneutical method he advances as by his description of "what actually takes place in every event of understanding."[20] And this he likens unto what happens in really genuine conversation, for he takes understanding itself to be a form of dialogue.

When two persons are engaged in true conversation, the relation between them does, of course, represent a complete inversion of the master-slave relationship, for neither is seeking to dominate the other: on the contrary, each is seeking to be fully *open* to and to *listen* to the other. To be sure, each of the conversation-partners lives and moves and has his being within his own horizon: each has his or her own established ways of construing experience, and these will not be merely suspended for the sake of the exchange. But, in the degree to which the conversation has real depth and seriousness, the cross-questioning that goes back and forth will entail each partner's conception of how the world is ordered being submitted to stringent interrogation which, as it progressively deepens, brings the interlocutors ever nearer that moment in which a real "fusion of horizons" may occur. This, for Gadamer, is the moment of understanding, the moment in which the whole hermeneutical effort wins through at last to fulfillment. And it is on the basis of this fundamental premise that his entire theory of interpretation stands.

Now Mikhail Bakhtin, Paul Ricoeur, and Hans-Georg Gadamer do most assuredly form a highly diverse group (which, if space permitted, I should enlarge by speaking also of Wayne Booth, whose important book, *Critical Understanding: The Powers and Limits of Pluralism,* bears very immediately on my general theme). Yet, for all the divergences of interest and doctrine

20. "Editor's Introduction," in Hans-Georg Gadamer, *Philosophical Hermeneutics,* trans. and ed. David E. Linge (Berkeley: University of California Press, 1977), p. xxvi.

that they reflect when considered together, they do present a significant unanimity in their principled hospitality to difference and variety in the cultural forums of the modern world. Indeed, they make us feel—and this is perhaps what is most quickening—that they conceive the health of the kind of *polis* we are given in this late time to be guaranteed above all else by difference and variety freely submitting themselves to a morality of mutual respect. And it is toward the end of promoting such a morality that they urge that cultural discourse be obedient to the dialogical principle.

I do not, of course, speak of these men because they offer anything like the kind of pony for teaching that was once offered in the great textbook by Cleanth Brooks and Robert Penn Warren, *Understanding Poetry* (with its critical introductions to a vast number of poetic texts and its "exercises" for the classroom and its various other "aids"). Indeed, I make an assumption rather different altogether from that of Brooks and Warren regarding the basic issue to be faced in the conduct of literary education. For them, at least as it seems to me, the matter was relatively simple: it was wholly an affair of mastering the techniques necessary for inculcating in students the habit of "close reading" of "the words on the page"—and thus literary study was considered to be a field quite separate and distinct from history and philosophy and the various other humanistic disciplines. But I find myself prompted toward a somewhat different view. No doubt the young people whom I face in the classroom need as desperately to be taught how to read "the words on the page" as did the student generation for which the famous Brooks-Warren textbooks *(Understanding Poetry, Understanding Fiction, Modern Rhetoric)* were prepared, and for this these books can still be enormously useful. But, then, once students begin in some measure to command the art of reading, they also need to be rescued from their impulse (quickened, as I suggest, by their supposition that the literary experience yields essentially religious satisfactions) prematurely to abdicate from a truly dialogical relationship with the text at hand for the sake of some essentially forensic manoeuvre. And, as I have wanted further to suggest, if this habit goes unchallenged, the literary classroom will have failed to prepare them, as in some degree it can, to live effectively in such a pluralistic culture as that which forms our present environment, where the conduct of life is everywhere dependent upon our carefully *listening* to the many voices and messages constituting the great polyphony of the age.

So my proposal is simply that an essential *praeparatio* for the teaching of literature in an age of carnival will consist not so much in the adoption of the kinds of critical strategies that Brooks and Warren were commending a generation ago (useful as they no doubt continue to be) as in the establishment in the classroom of such an ethos and atmosphere as will encourage young people not merely to read *with patience* "the words on the page" but also to consent to be "read by" *Daniel Deronda* or "The Wreck of the Deutschland" or *The Death of Ivan Ilych* or whatever else of real weight and importance they are confronting. Which is to say that literary pedagogy may need to begin not so much with questions of procedure at the level of practical criticism as with the hermeneutical problem, with the question as to which basic concept of the interpretative act *as such* will best offer one's students the kind of liberty that, in preparing them for the literary transaction, will also prepare them for the larger cultural transactions to which they will be summoned in the modern *polis*. And, furthermore, I am proposing that this will be a hermeneutic that, in inviting them to give their suffrage to the dialogical principle, will assist them in cultivating the virtue of Negative Capability—such a hermeneutic as is variously represented by Bakhtin and Ricoeur and Gadamer (and Wayne Booth). I am suggesting, in other words, that literary pedagogy needs at bottom to be grounded not only in literary but also in philosophical discipline (which is where I take it that hermeneutics is to be located). And this, of course, is a consideration that leads off into the further question as to how those who are preparing to teach literature in our colleges and universities ought themselves to be trained, for philosophical disciplines are notably absent in the curricula of graduate programs in English in American universities. Indeed, not since the appearance nearly forty years ago of that remarkable Novum Organum in the field of literary studies which René Wellek and

Austin Warren issued under the title *Theory of Literature* (1949) can I even recollect any discussion at all of the English graduate school comparable in weight and seriousness to their concluding chapter on "The Study of Literature in the Graduate School." Which reminds me of the small amazement that is made by the habitualness with which our faculties somnambulate their way through their business from year to year. But, were a searchlight to be turned on the doctoral program, surely the question would have to be raised as to how it can be adequately administered without any requirement in philosophical studies being set.

When my colleagues in the English Department at the University of Virginia decided a few years ago to woo the philosopher Richard Rorty, it was, as they said, because they needed a philosopher around "to keep them honest"—and what was meant by this was that large philosophical claims of one kind or another are implicitly being made in all systematic theory of literature, and such claims need to be fully aired and carefully examined. In helping his colleagues to do this Mr. Rorty is now performing a valuable service; but, happily, his central interests in recent years have come to focus on hermeneutical questions, and it is through his explorations of this whole range of things that he is making, as a philosopher, perhaps his most important contribution to the department. And so, I believe, it ought to go in other departments across the land, so that, with room being made for hermeneutical theory in the graduate program, prospective teachers of literature may be given a chance to reflect on how, prior to all procedures of practical criticism, the students whom they will eventually be teaching may themselves be given a chance at the largest kind of literary experience— not by way of assigned "exercises" of the sort that Brooks and Warren were prescribing a generation ago but by way of the establishment of the sorts of fundamental "assumptions" and the kind of classroom atmosphere that will encourage a truly dialogical relationship with that which is awaiting the event of understanding. It may not be expected, however, that the prospective teacher will, somehow or other, simply pick up the requisite sophistications after being thrust into preceptorials as a teaching assistant. No, he or she will need, I think, to have been offered some tutelage in the field of inquiry which is named after that son of Zeus and Maia—Hermes—who was the herald and messenger of the gods atop Mount Olympus and who, in conferring the gift of language, assisted humankind in transmuting what might otherwise have been beyond understanding into forms encompassable by human intelligence.

Women, Teaching, History

BARBARA JOHNSON

Deconstruction, Feminism, and Pedagogy

It is better to fail in teaching what should not be taught than to succeed in teaching what is not true.

Paul de Man

The old folks say, "It's not how little we know that hurts so, but that so much of what we know ain't so."

Toni Cade Bambara

The purpose of this essay is to articulate deconstruction and feminism in terms of pedagogical theory and practice—to make a link, in a sense, between epistemology and ideology, between "what is not true" and "what ain't so." My remarks will be based on two texts: an essay by Paul de Man (from which the first epigraph is taken) entitled "The Resistance to Theory,"[1] and a recent collection of essays on pedagogy, *Gendered Subjects,* edited by Margo Culley and Catherine Portuges.[2]

1. *The Pedagogical Imperative: Teaching as a Literary Genre,* ed. Barbara Johnson (New Haven: Yale University Press, 1982). Hereafter referred to as *PI.*
2. *Gendered Subjects: The Dynamics of Feminist Teaching,* ed. Margo Culley and Catherine Portuges (Boston: Routledge and Kegan Paul, 1985). Hereafter referred to as *GS.*

67

I will begin by reinserting the first epigraph into its original context. Speaking about the question of whether theory and scholarship are compatible, de Man writes:

A question arises only if a tension develops between methods of understanding and the knowledge which those methods allow one to reach. If there is indeed something about literature, as such, which allows for a discrepancy between truth and method, between *Wahrheit* and *Methode,* then scholarship and theory are no longer necessarily compatible; as a first casualty of this complication, the notion of "literature as such" as well as the clear distinction between history and interpretation can no longer be taken for granted. For a method that cannot be made to suit the "truth" of its object can only teach delusion . . . These uncertainties are manifest in the hostility directed at theory in the name of ethical and aesthetic values . . . The most effective of these attacks will denounce theory as an obstacle to scholarship and, consequently, to teaching. It is worth examining whether, and why, this is the case. For if this is indeed so, then it is better to fail in teaching what should not be taught than to succeed in teaching what is not true.   (*PI,* p. 4)

In order to make some headway with this assertion, it might be helpful to examine the ways in which de Man's essay itself functions pedagogically. What, if anything, does the essay teach? Interestingly, it opens by placing itself under the sign of failure.

This essay was not originally intended to address the question of teaching directly, although it was supposed to have a didactic and an educational function—which it failed to achieve.   (*PI,* p. 3)

The essay itself, in other words, can be read as an *enactment* of the failure to teach that it promotes. De Man explains that the essay was commissioned to provide a summary of recent work in literary theory for an MLA volume entitled *Introduction to Scholarship in Modern Languages and Literatures.* "I found it difficult to live up, in minimal good faith, to the requirements of this program, and could only try to explain, as concisely as possible, why the main theoretical interest of literary theory consists in the impossibility of its definition. The Committee rightly judged that this was an inauspicious way to achieve the pedagogical objectives of the volume and commissioned another article." It is not pedagogically auspicious, it seems, to be sent on a mission of scholarship and to come back with a tale of impossibility. Yet it is the value of such a failure to teach that de Man is asserting as the moral of his pedagogical tale. What is of pedagogical interest for him is precisely what resists pedagogical mastery.

Feminist theories of pedagogy, too, involve a critique of masterful meaning and an interest in the resistance to reductive appropriation. One of the most visible differences, however, lies in the status of the pedagogical subject. De Man makes a clear case for teaching as an impersonal rather than an interpersonal phenomenon:

Overfacile opinion notwithstanding, teaching is not primarily an intersubjective relationship between people but a cognitive process in which self and other are only tangentially and contiguously involved. The only teaching worthy of the name is scholarly, not personal. (*PI*, p. 3)

When de Man ultimately concludes that the resistance to theory is ineradicable because theory is its own self-resistance, that self-resistance is also a form of resistance to the very notion of a self.

The title *Gendered Subjects,* on the other hand, indicates a move to reverse the impersonalization that de Man radicalizes and to reintroduce the personal, or at least the positional, as a way of disseminating authority and decomposing the false universality of patriarchally institutionalized meanings. Not only has female personal experience tended to be excluded from the discourse of knowledge, but the realm of the personal itself has been coded as female and devalued for that reason. In opposition, therefore, many of the essays of the volume consciously assume a first-person autobiographical stance toward the question of pedagogical theory: this is how it looks *to me* as the only black woman in an English department, or as a male feminist, or as a teacher of feminist theory. This is where I am positioned in the institutions of pedagogy. Explicitly speaking from *where one is* turns out to allow for an expansion rather than a contraction of the range of pedagogical experiences available. While de Man urges maximum abstraction, Michele Russell, for one, exhorts us to "use everything":

The size and design of the desks, for example. They are wooden, with one-sided stationary writing arms attached. The embodiment of a poor school. Small. Unyielding. Thirty years old. Most of the black women [students] are ample-bodied . . . Sitting there for one hour—not to mention trying to concentrate and work—is a contortionist's miracle, or a stoic's. It feels like getting left back.

With desks as a starting-point for thinking about our youths in school, class members are prompted to recall the mental state such seats encouraged. They cite awkwardness, restlessness, and furtive embarrassment. When they took away our full-top desks with interior compartments, we remembered how *exposed* we felt . . . We talk about all the unnecessary, but deliberate, ways the educational process is made uncomfortable for the poor . . . We remember that one reason many of us stopped going to school was that it became an invasion of privacy. (*GS*, p. 163)

The constraints of positionality here *literally* become the access route to a whole rethinking of the educational enterprise. This, too, is a story of the pedagogical recuperation of a failure of teaching, but in a very different sense from de Man's.

I find both these versions of the resistance to pedagogy equally compelling and equally difficult to put into genuine—as opposed to apparent—practice. Both versions involve an imperative not to lose, but rather to work through, that resistance. The question I want to ask here is whether there is a *simple* incompatibility between the depersonalization of deconstruction and the re-personalization of feminism, or whether each is not in reality haunted by the ghost of the other.

The personal in fact returns in de Man in two very different ways. On the one hand, he has always been and is increasingly being lionized as the embodiment of the great teacher: the recent issue of *Yale French Studies* entitled *The Lesson of Paul de Man* (1985) opens by saying, "He was never not teaching." Testimonials repeatedly assert that it was precisely his way of denying personal authority that engendered the unique power of his personal authority. What is not clear, of course, is whether his personal impact should be seen as a sign of the success or of the failure of his pedagogical project as he conceived it. Another sign of this paradox is the function of proper names in the present essay: the name of de Man occupies a focal position that no proper name assumes—and this is part of the point—in the feminist collective volume, however personal the narratives. (Is it by chance, moreover, that he should be named "the Man"?)

The other return of the personal in de Man's work takes a rhetorical form. Even a cursory perusal of his essays reveals that their insistent rhetorical mode—in the service of their irony, paradoxes, and chiasmuses—is personification. In the absence of a personal agent of signification, the rhetorical entities themselves are constantly said to "know," to "renounce," or to "resign themselves" in the place where the poet or critic as subject has disappeared. It is as though the operations of personhood could not be eliminated but only transferred—which does not necessarily imply that their rightful place is within the self. Rather, it implies that personification is a trope available for occupancy by either subjects or linguistic entities, the difference between them being ultimately indeterminable if each is known only in and through a text. The teacher, in any event, becomes neither impersonal nor personal: the agent of pedagogy is a personification.

What the transfer of personhood to rhetorical entities does enable de Man to achieve, however, is an elimination of sexual difference. By making personhood the property of an "it," de Man is able to claim a form of universality which can be said to inhere in language itself, and which is not directly subject to ordinary feminist critique, however gender-inflected language can in fact be shown to be. The analysis of the rhetorical operations of self-resistance is, as de Man asserts, irrefutable in its own terms. But the question *can* be asked why de Man's discourse of self-resistance and uncertainty has achieved such authority and visibility, while the self-resistance and uncertainty of *women* have been part of what has insured their lack of authority and their invisibility. It would seem that one has to be positioned in the place of power in order for one's self-resistance to be valued. Self-resistance, indeed, may be one of the few viable postures remaining for the white male establishment.

But does this imply that the task of feminism would be the overcoming of self-resistance? In many of the essays in *Gendered Subjects* this would seem to be the case. A typical essay (this one by Susan Stanford Friedman) begins: "I choose to address the issue of feminist pedagogy in a personal narrative not only because the cornerstone of that pedagogy has been the validation of experience, but also because my own evolution as a teacher in a university setting over the last twelve years illuminates a pedagogical problem we all must face." (*GS*, p. 203). What is interesting about this attempt at personalization is how quickly it slides into an assumption of generalizability ("a problem we all must face"). The recourse to "experience" is always, in these essays, a double-edged sword. On the one hand, it would be impossible to deny that female experience has been undervalidated. On the other hand, the moment one assumes one knows what female experience is, one runs the risk of creating another reductive appropriation—an appropriation that consists in the reduction of experience *as* self-resistance. While deconstructive discourse may be in danger of overvaluing self-resistance, feminist discourse may be in danger of losing self-resistance as a source of insight and power rather than merely of powerlessness. While de Man's writing is haunted by the return of personification, feminist writing is haunted by the return of abstraction. The challenge facing both approaches is to recognize these ghosts not as external enemies but as the uncannily familiar strangers that make their own knowledge both possible and problematic.[3]

3. This essay first appeared in my recent book entitled *A World of Difference* (Baltimore: The Johns Hopkins University Press, 1987) and is reprinted by permission of the publisher.

DEBORAH EPSTEIN NORD

Mill and Ruskin on the
Woman Question Revisited

As a student and teacher of nineteenth-century literature I find it both imperative and fascinating to consider literary texts within their historical contexts. This has often meant that my students are asked to read about Manchester in order to discuss *Mary Barton,* to understand something about urban crime and prostitution as a background to *Oliver Twist,* to have some conception of the place of the Jew in Victorian society in order to tackle *Daniel Deronda.* These are, in some sense, obvious ways to bring material history to bear on literature, and Victorian texts in particular invite this kind of inquiry. The study of Victorianism has, in fact, been an almost automatically interdisciplinary enterprise, with an often indistinguishable line dividing the historian's work from that of the literary critic.

There are, however, other ways to introduce history into the field of literary study, and one of these is to locate literary texts within ideological debate and to recognize ideological debate as an ever-changing part of history. Texts themselves have a specific relationship to contemporary phenomena—be they as specific as the French Revolution or as amorphous as changing class or family configurations—but *readers* are also placed ideologically in time and respond accordingly. I want to make students aware of the special relationship of critical response to

73

historically bound fluctuations in taste, values, and political opinions. The interdependent histories of critical response and ideology can be illustrated with a few easily recognizable examples from Victorian literature: the mid-twentieth-century rejection of Carlyle because of a posthumous association with fascism, the reassessment of Dickens' fiction in the light of psychoanalytic thought that began with Edmund Wilson in the 1940s, the rediscovery of Elizabeth Barrett Browning's narrative poem, *Aurora Leigh,* as a result of late-twentieth century feminism. To remind students of these particular kinds of shifts in critical opinion is to suggest to them that *they* exist within history just as texts do, and to encourage in them the potential both for critical distance and for a personal engagement with literature. I want to suggest here how students might be brought to see themselves and the texts they read as part of a many-layered process of evolving analysis, and I will take as my example the revival and yoking of two Victorian texts: John Ruskin's *Sesame and Lilies* (1865) and John Stuart Mill's *The Subjection of Women* (1869).

It was Kate Millett who first brought these texts together for twentieth-century consideration in her pioneering and controversial work of feminist criticism, *Sexual Politics* (1969). *Sesame and Lilies,* a very popular volume among Ruskin's contemporaries, had been largely ignored in our own century except, as Millett reminds us, by Walter Houghton, who identified it as " 'the most important single document . . . for the characteristic idealization of love, women, and the home in Victorian thought.' "[1] Mill's *Subjection,* although taken up by nineteenth- and early twentieth-century suffragists as a sacred text, was roundly criticized by contemporary reviewers as social heresy and largely unread by twentieth-century students of Mill who gravitated instead to the more canonical *On Liberty, Utilitar-*

---

1. Kate Millett, *Sexual Politics* (Garden City: Doubleday, 1970), p. 89. A visitor to Harvard's Widener Library will be surprised to find at least thirty editions of *Sesame and Lilies* listed in the card catalogue. Many of these editions are American, and the history of this text's American reception in the late nineteenth century would be interesting to trace.

ianism, or *On Representative Government.*[2] (I cannot say with absolute certainty that the *Subjection* was introduced into curricula only after 1970, but I have in front of me an M.I.T. paperback edition that first appeared in 1970 and was reprinted eight times between that date and 1982. It has a peculiarly dated cover featuring a presumably "liberated" couple of the early 1970s.)

Millett characterized the two views of women espoused by Ruskin and Mill as, respectively, the "chivalric" and the "rational." Ruskin preached the repressive and regressive opinion that the good of society depended on woman's special link with the Natural and on her cultivation of those aspects of her inborn character that complemented man's less organic, more culturally bound nature. Woman's special gift was for "self-renunciation" rather than "self-development," and her special mission the preservation of the hearth as a shrine of sacredness and peace.[3] Mill, on the other hand, argued that woman's subordinate position in society and in the home represented a status quo that had nothing to do with *nature* and was no more inevitable than other retrograde social institutions such as slavery. In fact, he went so far as to see in marriage a form of "domestic slavery," and in the home no haven of serenity, but a reign of despotism. Mill also maintained that the character of woman was undefinable because of what he called the "hot-house and stove cultivation" of her nature, because of "forced repression in some directions, unnatural stimulation in others."[4] Millett praised Mill especially for his psychological insight and for its grounding in a "more lucid distinction between prescription and description than one encounters in Freud."[5]

Acknowledging the sobering fact that my students were infants in 1969, I try, first of all, to put Millett's treatment of Mill

2. See Millett, *Sexual Politics,* p. 92, for outraged responses to Mill's *Subjection.*

3. John Ruskin, *Sesame and Lilies* (London: Merrill and Baker, 1888), pp. 102–103.

4. John Stuart Mill, *The Subjection of Women* (Cambridge, Mass.: M.I.T. Press, 1970), p. 22.

5. Millett, *Sexual Politics,* p. 95.

and Ruskin in its historical and ideological context: squarely in the midst of the renaissance of modern feminism we call the Women's Liberation Movement. She found a villain in Ruskin because he seemed to her the precursor of theorists like Erik Erikson—to whom she devotes ten pages of her book—who celebrate woman's biological and presumed psychological difference from men as a socially and politically useful force. Seeing anatomy as woman's fortuitous destiny Erikson offers the idea of her "inner space" as a wellspring of creativity and deep feeling.[6] Ruskin also appeared to Millett as the partial creator of a myth of marriage that had reached its apotheosis in the 1950s and against which the feminists of the sixties fought bitterly. The mystique of femininity and the sexual division of labor within marriage and outside of it were the bugbears of the women's movement from within which Millett wrote.

If Ruskin could play the villain in this plot, then Mill could take the role of prophetic hero. Millett championed his vision of an egalitarian, companionate marriage and his emphasis on the fundamental sameness of men and women out of which such egalitarianism might grow. His vision seemed to her "full of a new and promising vigor," as new and promising for the 1970s as for the 1870s. It was above all Mill's insistence on emancipation through rights and law, whether in the public or the private sphere, that made him so important to the feminist sensibility of the late 1960s. Mill had declared the private realm subject to public rule and invited law into the domestic sphere to enforce equality between husband and wife; the women's movement insisted with him that the personal was political and the hearth in need of exposure to the air of law and standards of equal justice.

Having suggested to students that Millett's Mill and Ruskin were the Mill and Ruskin of 1969 and of the salad days of the women's movement, I would next want them to resurrect the sages of the *1860s* and reconstruct the actual Victorian debate that she had uncovered for us. This is not to suggest that Millett had got it wrong or missed some essential truth, but simply that,

6. See Millett, *Sexual Politics,* pp. 210–220. Erikson's article "Womanhood and the Inner Space" first appeared in *Daedalus* in the spring of 1964.

as should by now be obvious, each age creates or recreates certain debates for itself and that the terms of any given debate are more or less accessible to us at any given moment in history. The popularity of Ruskin's terms in the nineteenth century and their relative odiousness to the twentieth-century feminist reader generates certain historical and philosophical questions for us. Because Mill's perspective seems, at first glance, so much more compatible with our own, I would make an effort to place *Ruskin* within a more interesting and complex context of thought than might at first be obvious.

The rise of the leisured middle class and the freeing of women of that class from time-consuming domestic work or production within the home presented mid-nineteenth-century social critics with a question about the future role of women. If some women had the time to do something *besides* basic home labor and child-rearing, what should they undertake to do? The possibility of educating women formally engaged the attention of both Ruskin and Mill, although they disagreed about the goals and content of such education. The question of work outside the home inspired some critics and confounded or vexed others. While Mill tried to imagine women's futures in much the same way he thought about the rights and opportunities available to men, Ruskin and others envisioned women's natural domestic talents expanding into a widening female influence that would benefit all of society. Indeed, the approach of each of these men to the "woman question" is wholly consistent with their general approaches to wider social issues: Mill's liberalism moves him to look toward democracy, law, and education to answer the question about women, and Ruskin's idiosyncratic brand of radico-conservatism weds him to a notion of the organic growth of woman's traditionally benign and nurturing influence.

For Mill, both as general social critic and as defender of female emancipation, the ultimate enemy is the tyranny of the powerful over the powerless, the vocal over the silent, the en-franchised over the disenfranchised; Ruskin's enemies in *Sesame and Lilies* and elsewhere are the materialism and mammonism of Victorian society. If we read not just the "Lilies" section of Ruskin's work but also the "Sesame" section, we see quite clearly why he imagines a traditional notion of the "feminine" as the one thing needful, as the antidote to a wrongheaded, male-created world. The world he sees before him suffers from "the insanity of avarice": the people have turned into a "money-making mob" and lost their capacity for understanding and sympathy.[7] Vulgarity has supplanted true passion, and greed has eclipsed the glory of work itself. "But now," Ruskin admonishes his audience, "having no true business, we pour our whole *masculine* energy into the false business of money-making; and having no true emotion, we must have false emotions dressed up for us to play with."[8] He has set the stage for the praise of *feminine* energy, and he will use it both as a stick to beat the avaricious mob of men and as a prod to keep women in line and in the home.

What emerges from a careful reading of Ruskin's text, then, is the centrality of the ideal feminine to a certain critique of individualism and of the capitalist ethic that depends on it. By teaching *Sesame and Lilies* in conjunction with Dickens' *Dombey and Son,* as I have recently done, I try to make accessible to students what might otherwise elude them: the dependence of Victorian social critics on an idealized, self-abnegating, even Christlike femininity to expose the faults of a self-interested, exploitative, life-denying masculinity. Millett herself refers to *Dombey* as the novel in which Dickens achieves a "nearly perfect indictment of both patriarchy and capitalism" without ever "relinquishing the sentimental version of women" that is to be found in Ruskin.[9] What Millett misses, I think, is that Ruskin is making the very same indictment, and that Dickens makes it not in spite of his worship of self-sacrificing femity but by virtue of it, using it as a powerful basis for the prosecution. In *Dombey* the principle of femininity—with its links to nature and the maternal, to the sea and to the wife who dies giving birth in the first pages of the novel—is that element which Mr. Dombey, at great risk to himself, tries so hard to repress; and only in allowing the feminine to resurface in the form of his daughter Florence can Mr. Dombey be redeemed. "Dombey

---

7. Ruskin, *Sesame and Lilies,* pp. 48–49.

8. Ruskin, *Sesame and Lilies,* p. 67 (emphasis added).

9. Millett, *Sexual Politics,* pp. 89–90.

and Son" has to become "Dombey and Daughter" and the "house" of Dombey a home rather than a firm.

The placing of woman at the center of a critique of capitalist society depends, in the cases of both Ruskin and Dickens, upon a fairly rigid philosophy of sexual difference and acceptance of the notion of separate spheres. Students chafe at this just as Kate Millett did (although Florence Dombey appeals to them because of her courage and suffering in a way that Ruskin's hypothetical angels on the hearth do not); so it is my task to make them aware of one more nuance of Victorian history. Ruskin's views provided some contemporary women with a justification for expanding their sphere of labor and influence from the home into the community, while preserving those virtues of service and self-sacrifice that Ruskin saw as uniquely their own. Victorian women who sought careers in nursing, public health, social work, and teaching often took advantage of a Ruskinian philosophy of separate spheres to claim a public forum for the exercise of "private" and traditionally womanly skills; and the rhetoric of essentialism—of insisting on the inherent nature of sexual difference—informed a number of strains of nineteenth-century and early twentieth-century feminist discourse, from suffragism to feminist pacifism.[10] If Ruskin preached feminine superiority, at least in certain realms, why not claim that superiorty as a source of real power, particularly when sources of power were so limited? As promoter of education for women and benefactor to those like Octavia Hill who pioneered in the field of social work, Ruskin was considered by many to be a friend of the nineteenth-century women's movement.

The irony of Ruskin's position on women, with its seemingly obvious datedness, is that not only have we not transcended the terms of his debate in the 1980s, but we have returned to them with a vengeance. The questions of sexual difference and of essentialism, which lie stubbornly at the center of *Sesame and Lilies,* mean more to the reader of the 1980s than they did to Kate Millett or to the reader of the 1960s. Intellectually, and

10. See Jeffrey L. Spear, *Dreams of an English Eden: Ruskin and His Tradition in Social Criticism* (New York: Columbia University Press, 1984), pp. 167–177, for Ruskin's influence on female philanthropy.

perhaps politically, we are more concerned with the subject of sexual difference than with Millett's "equal justice," more preoccupied with the nature and causes of difference than with the external impediments to equality and emancipation. Although students reject Ruskin's extreme essentialism and the patronizing tone of his celebration of feminine virtue, they are far more engaged by the issues he raises than by Mill's call for equality within the home and within society, perhaps because they take Mill's point of view for granted, perhaps because they are absorbed in the ideological drift of the moment. Although students may never have read Helen Cixous or Julia Kristeva, they are familiar with the debates that such theorists have created within feminism.

When, in class discussion, Victorian concerns with sexual difference begin to dovetail with related concerns in contemporary feminist theory, students detect an interesting contradiction in Mill's refusal to define the nature of woman. On the one hand we have his radical statement that the knowledge men have of women is and will be "wretchedly imperfect and superficial . . . until women themselves have told all that they have to tell" and, on the other, we have the following passage on which, I should add, all of my students seem to focus:

A woman seldom runs wild after an abstraction. The habitual direction of her mind to dealing with things as individuals rather than in groups, and (what is closely connected with it) her more lively interest in the present feelings of persons . . . these two things make her extremely unlikely to put faith in any speculation which loses sight of individuals . . . Women's thoughts are thus as useful in giving reality to those of thinking men, as men's thoughts in giving width and largeness to those of women.[11]

A number of things emerge from this passage: first, Mill insists on identifying something presumably inherent in female nature even though he has claimed the impossibility of doing so accurately; second, he seems to be proposing some notion of complementary opposition between the sexes that is not unlike Ruskin's; and third, the very characteristics he attributes to

11. Mill, *Subjection*, p. 59.

female nature are both clichéd (women care about people, men care about ideas) and strikingly familiar from recent feminist explorations of gender difference.

After students get over the initial pleasure of having caught Mill in a contradiction, they are reminded very quickly of the psychologist Carol Gilligan's recent, immensely popular book, *In a Different Voice,* in which she argues that girls have a sense of justice that grows out of their concern for individual circumstances and not out of abstract principles of right and wrong.[12] Gilligan is interested in showing that models of psychological and particularly moral development have heretofore been based on male experience and that the behavior and thought of females have been devalued and found wanting because they were measured against this standard. What, I ask students, is the difference between Mill's assessment of gender difference and Gilligan's? Between Mill's and Ruskin's? Ruskin's and Gilligan's? It is not at all my intention to collapse the differences but rather to use points of similarity as a way of making sharper distinctions.

In making these distinctions students inevitably encounter the epistemological problem of opposition and its relationship to hierarchy. Can there be a positing of gender differences without a sense of the primacy of one gender over the other? Perhaps Gilligan can achieve this, perhaps Mill cannot. If we look at Cixous' *La jeune née* we find an absolute rejection of the possibility of binary oppositions *without* hierarchical implications and, further, the assertion that such oppositions (Activity/Passivity, Sun/Moon, Culture/Nature, Head/Heart, and so on) always refer back to the fundamental couple or coupling of Male/Female.[13] She sees the inescapability of what one recent critic has called "patriarchal binary thought" and the inevitability, given the existence of such thought, of the valuing of masculine principles over female ones.[14]

12. Carol Gilligan, *In a Different Voice* (Cambridge, Mass.: Harvard University Press, 1982).

13. See excerpts from *La jeune née* in Elaine Marks and Isabelle de Courtivron, *New French Feminisms* (New York: Schocken, 1981), especially pp. 90–93. See also Toril Moi, *Sexual/Textual Politics: Feminist Literary Theory* (London: Methuen, 1985), pp. 104–105.

14. Moi, *Sexual/Textual Politics,* p. 104.

Acknowledging the inescapability of such hierarchal thought
and language, Julia Kristeva, another theorist who has dealt
with the problems of difference, has asserted that woman does
not exist, that there is no real place for her within patriarchal
thought (except on the margins), and that "femininity" or "the
feminine" cannot be defined or identified.[15] Kristeva's "uncom-
promising anti-essentialism"[16] echoes that part of Mill's *Subjection* that finds the real nature of woman elusive and indecipherable
and sees only an absence, a void, where an authentic identity
should be. Students grasp this unexpected correspondence and,
in so doing, recognize both the validity and the danger of suggesting that woman's identity is unknowable.

Still other feminist theorists, searching for the ultimate source
of difference, consider the body and play with the notion that
female writing, for instance, might express or inscribe the body
with its undeniable difference. Helene Cixous imagines a total
redefining of the words "feminine" and "masculine" that would
undo layers of cultural constraint and confusion and build, instead, out of the body:

To predict what will happen to sexual difference—in another time (in
two or three hundred years) is impossible. But there should be no
misunderstanding: men and women are caught up in a network of
millennial cultural determinations of a complexity that is practically
unanalyzable . . . There is no reason to exclude the possibility of radical transformation of behavior, mentalities, roles, and political economy . . . Let us imagine simultaneously a *general* change in all of the
structures . . . and a transformation of our relationship to our body . . .[17]

Cixous envisions woman's return to her body and her creation
of a new kind of culture and writing that will be inseparable
from it. What is the connection, vexed as it may be, between
the "inner space" of Erikson and the more free-floating and
utopian biologism of Cixous? Is Cixous subverting Ruskin, or
is she rewriting him?

15. See the excerpt from *"La femme, ce n'est jamais ça"* in *New French
Feminisms*, pp. 137–138; and Moi, *Sexual/Textual Politics*, pp. 163–167.
16. Moi, *Sexual/Textual Politics*, p. 164.
17. From *La jeune née*, in Marks and de Courtivron, *New French Feminisms*,
pp. 96–97.

One more visible sign that we have returned, in however altered a way, to Ruskin's interest in sexual difference is the reappearance of Freud—and psychoanalytic theory in general—at the center of much feminist theory, literary or otherwise. Whereas Millett rejected Freudian theory almost completely, preferring Mill's psychology to Freud's and blaming Freud for the notion of biological determinism, recent critics have felt the need to grapple with psychoanalytic theory, in large part because it is still one of the most cogent ways to get at the question of sexual difference and its origins.[18]

What might appear to be an odd mingling of texts—Ruskin and Cixous, Mill and Kristeva, Dickens and Erikson, Millett and Freud—serves, I hope, to make the pedagogical point I am after. It is not enough to teach that literary texts are rooted in a historical moment and exist in the context of a material and social history: we must also suggest that readers exist in history and that, for that reason, literary texts are forever changing.

18. See, for instance, Nancy Chodorow's *The Reproduction of Mothering: Psychoanalysis and the Sociology of Gender* (Berkeley: University of California Press, 1978), a landmark work in the recent scholarship on gender difference.

Retrospect and Prospect

J. HILLIS MILLER

The Function of Rhetorical Study at the Present Time

*The new statement is always hated by the old, and,
to those dwelling in the old, comes like an abyss
of scepticism. But the eye soon gets wonted to it,
for the eye and it are effects of one cause; then its
innocency and benefit appear, and presently, all
of its energies spent, it pales and dwindles before
the revelation of the new hour.*

    Emerson, "Circles"

    What is the present relation between literary theory and pe-
dagogy in American colleges and universities? Most professors
in departments of literature still assume that their chief respon-
sibility is teaching students how to read "primary texts." The
context or situation in which that duty is performed, however,
has changed radically from what it was thirty years ago. The
old consensus in literary studies in the United States, such as it
was, has been challenged in manifold ways. There is now, for
example, widespread disagreement about just what those "primary" texts ought to be and about just how they ought to be
organized in courses and curricula. At the same time, as everyone knows, there has been a spectacular proliferation of powerful and incompatible "critical theories": structuralist, semiotic,
Lacanian, Marxist, reader-response, deconstructionist, New
Historicist, and so on.

    In such a situation the relation of "theory" to "example" is
fundamentally changed. Changed also is the relation of theory
to the act of reading the example, as well as the relation of that

whole process to what may be called, by a kind of shorthand, "history." I mean here by "history" something assumed to be radically different from either theory or literary texts. History takes place in the real world of flesh and blood men and women carrying on their daily lives. We might mean by history in this sense something that occurred either in the past or now, when, as we say, "history is being made every day." I believe we tend to think these days of the historical as violent, as involving suffering. The downing of Korean Flight 007 is more likely to come to mind as an example of a historical happening than the "blameless" lives of an insurance salesperson in Topeka, Kansas, and his or her spouse and children.

All reading and teaching of literature is theoretical. This is so in the strict sense that any sort of reading and teaching of literature presupposes all sorts of assumptions about what literature is and about how it should be read. I mean by "literary theory" here the shift from the hermeneutical process of identifying the meaning of a work of literature to a focus on the question of how that meaning is generated. When there is a general consensus about literary theory, for example at the time the New Criticism was more or less universally accepted in the United States, theory tends to be effaced, latent, presupposed; one just goes to work doing or teaching "close reading." When a multitude of conflicting critical theories call for attention, however, and when in addition there is confusion over the canons and the curricula of literature, as at the present time, then literary theory, rather than being something that can more or less be taken for granted, becomes overt, exigent, even, some would say, strident. Theory tends to become a primary means of access to the works read. These works now tend to be redefined as "examples" demonstrating the productive effectiveness of this or that theory.

In such a situation, literary theory even tends to become a primary object of study in itself, as in that ever-increasing number of courses and programs these days in critical theory as such, sometimes treated historically, sometimes as a matter of current concern. The "examples" read, at the same time, are no longer so often drawn from an established canon arranged in traditional canonical ways, for example by genre and historical period. The result is that the examples read are likely to be subordinated to theory in the sense that the example is read as a more or less arbitrary choice among innumerable possible ones of a theoretical concept that claims universal applicability. The teacher teaches the student to read the example in a certain way. The implicit claim is that everything should be read analogously. What is taught is a universal way of reading and its accompanying explicit and self-conscious theory, not the works in an agreed-upon canon read in canonical ways as having established meanings and as transmitting from the past agreed-upon cultural values. The place of those established meanings and enshrined values is more and more taken by theory itself.

Seen from this perspective, the function of theory is to liberate us from ideology, even from the ideology of theory itself. Critical theory performs an ethical and political act. It has institutional and social force. Critical theory is, then, no longer "merely theoretical." Rather it makes something happen by disabling the power of the works read to go on proliferating the ideology that traditional canonical or thematic readings of it have blindly asserted, often without even being aware that they are merely thematic or are ideologically determined. Critical theory, seen from this point of view, earns its label of "critical." It becomes within our educational institutions one of the most powerful and indispensable means of unmasking ideological assumptions.[1]

That our profession is undergoing unusually rapid changes no one can doubt, especially those of us who find ourselves chair-

---

1. The essay that follows was originally presented at Texas A & M at a summer conference of the Association of Departments of English; it was printed in a special issue of the *ADE Bulletin,* 62 (Sept.-Nov.1979), *The State of the Discipline: 1970s–1980s.* Permission to reprint this essay is gratefully acknowledged. I have somewhat altered the essay to make it correspond better to my present convictions—for example, by the omission of a sentence about the canon—but the essay is still marked by its original occasion and by the time of its writing. As for the canon, I would now say that no canon is absolute. Each is an aspect of particular historical, ideological, political circumstances, both causer and caused, maker of history and made by it. Changes in the canon can come in two ways, however: by the addition of new works or the dropping of old ones, and, on the other hand, by new, noncanonical readings of old canonical works; for example, the challenging new feminist readings of Milton or of Victorian fiction.

men of departments of English. The pressures are coming from
various directions. Chairmen must often feel themselves to be
at the confluence of contradictory winds of change, blown here
and there like a tumbleweed. A chairman's response may be to
make himself or herself as much like a rock as possible, stolid
and imperturbable. The point of this paper is to assert that this
is the wrong strategy.

The changes are coming from society, in one direction, and
from within the discipline itself, in the other. Although they
appear to be contradictory or to make contradictory demands
on departments and on chairmen and governing committees, I
argue that this is not so and that the present situation offers us
an opportunity to revitalize literary study as well as the study
of expository writing.

One change is being imposed from outside the discipline, from
society. By society here I mean the context within which literary
study in America dwells, the context it serves and is served by:
parents, school boards, trustees, regents, legislatures, the
"media." We teachers of literature have fewer students already
and will apparently have still fewer as the years go by, both in
individual courses and as majors in the various departments of
literature. Those fewer are, we are told, steadily less well prepared, both in literature itself and in what are called "basic
language skills." They cannot write well. They cannot read well
either. The reading of works of literature appears every day to
be playing a less and less important role in our culture generally.
The complex social function performed in Elizabethan and Ja-
cobean England by going to the theater and in Victorian England by the reading of novels is performed these days by other
activities, mostly, so it seems, by watching television. The reading of a novel, a poem, or a play, or even the watching of a
play, is likely to become an increasingly artificial, marginal, or
archaic activity. It is beginning to seem more and more odd, to
some people, to be asked to take seriously the literature of a
small island on the edge of Europe, a small island, moreover,
that has ceased to be a major world power. It might be more
important to learn Russian, Chinese, or Arabic. At the same
time, American society has begun to recognize that we are to
a considerable degree a multilingual people, not only because

many of us have Spanish or some other tongue as a first language but because we speak and write many different forms of English besides the idiolect and grapholect of standard English. For better or worse, much "standard English as a second language" must be taught, even to college students.

As College Board scores go down from year to year, our society is demanding in a louder and louder chorus that schools and colleges do something about the inability of our young people to read and write. This demand, at the college and university level, is being made on professors who have been trained to teach the details of literary history and the intricacies of meaning in works by Shakespeare or Milton, Keats or Woolf. Even before they found themselves asked to teach more and more composition, many departments of English had been demoralized by declining enrollments and had begun to assign (or allow) their Shakespeareans and medievalists to teach classes in modern fiction, in film, or in continental novels in translation, just as the department of classics in one large state university justifies its existence at the undergraduate level by a lecture course on "mythology." A large proportion of the courses offered by the department of English in one good liberal arts college I visited recently included at least one work by J. L. Borges. This department is for all practical purposes a department of continental literature in translation, and the departments of Spanish, French, and German at the same college are small and ineffective.

In the area of expository writing a large industry is being mobilized to create a new discipline. This mobilization includes distinguished literary theorists and historians like E. D. Hirsch, Wayne Booth, and Stanley Fish, who began as literary critics, not as experts on the teaching of composition. At the same time, more and more bright young people are making careers in composition, seeking training in rhetoric, in linguistics, and in educational psychology, rather than limiting themselves to literary history and criticism. This is all to the good, but it will obviously weaken further the traditional activities of the study of literature as such.

At the same time, unusually rapid changes have been initiated from the other direction, from within the discipline of literary

study. Forty years ago the field of literary study in America was
more or less completely dominated by the method of intrinsic
reading called the New Criticism and by a positivistic literary
history committed to gathering facts and establishing texts. The
latter mode was associated with the method of scientific research. It descended from such nineteenth-century metaphorical
assimilations of literary study to scientific method as that of
Hippolyte Taine, as well as from the long European tradition
of philology and textual criticism originally coming from the
study of Greek and Latin literature and from biblical hermeneutics. The archetypal criticism of Northrop Frye was in 1948
just appearing as the first strong alternative to the New Criticism. There was a somewhat marginal presence of the great
German philological tradition in the form of refugee scholars
like Erich Auerbach and Leo Spitzer. Some news of continental
Formalism—Russian, Czech, and Polish—was seeping through
in the influential book by René Wellek and Austin Warren
called *The Theory of Literature.* In spite of the latter book,
however, literary study in America was still insular. It was a
more or less self-enclosed Anglo-American tradition, confident
that it could go on going it alone.

Today the situation is greatly changed. No serious student of
literature can fail to think of this discipline as an international
enterprise. It is just as important for the student of Chaucer,
of Shakespeare, or of Dickens to know about continental criticism and to read a journal like *Poetics Today,* which is edited
at the Institute for Poetics and Semiotics in Tel Aviv, as it is to
know the traditional English-language secondary works on these
authors or to read *PMLA.*

Moreover, the range of viable alternatives in literary methodology has become bafflingly large. These alternatives can, so
it seems, hardly be reconciled in some grand synthesis. *Il faut
choisir,* not in the sense that one is forced to become a disciple
of one or another of these schools, but in the sense that it is
impossible to combine them eclectically, taking a bit from one
and a bit from another, unless one is willing to settle for a large
measure of incoherence in one's thinking about literature and
one's teaching of it. Along with the still powerful New Criticism,
archetypal criticism, and positivistic literary history, there is a

more or less fully elaborated phenomenological or hermeneutic criticism, a "criticism of consciousness," as it is sometimes called. A new semiotic formalism inspired by linguistics has been developed. There is Structuralist criticism deriving from structural linguistics and structural anthropology. A powerful new form of psychoanalytic criticism, mostly imported from France, has become influential. A revived Marxist and sociological criticism is beginning to take strong hold in America. Another new kind of criticism focuses on reader response and on what is called in Germany *Rezeptiongeschichte*. There is, finally, a form of literary study that concentrates on the rhetoric of literary texts, taking rhetoric in the sense of the investigation of the role of figurative language in literature. This method is sometimes called "deconstruction," which as a name at least has the advantage of distinguishing this approach firmly from any form of "structuralism." It is associated with Jacques Derrida in France and with certain critics at Yale, as well as, increasingly, with younger critics at other colleges and universities in the United States, in England, and on the Continent. All these new forms are international in scope. The masterworks in each are as likely to have been written in Russian, German, French, or Italian as in English, and the delays and inadequacies of translation have made particular difficulties for literary study recently in America. Relatively few students and young teachers here can read even one foreign language fluently, much less the whole necessary panoply.

These facts are well known to all chairmen of departments of English these days. What is not so clear is the right responses to them. I have sometimes found myself agreeing with those who foresee the atrophy and perhaps eventual disappearance of traditional departments focused on English literary history. After all, such departments, whose main business is the interpretation of major English and American works, from *Beowulf* and Chaucer to Wallace Stevens or Robert Frost, have existed in something like their present form for less than a hundred years. Before that, major universities did without them. They could cease to exist, and the academies would do without them again. Literature departments could become small and marginal, as have departments of classics. Their place could be taken by large and vigorous pragmatic programs in expository writing.

I now no longer think this is at all likely, or at least not likely unless the professors of literary history and interpretation remain inflexibly committed to maintaining things as they are or have been. The analogy with classics is a false one. Whatever the virtues of Greek and Latin as the languages of major literatures or as the basis for so many centuries of prolonged masculine puberty rituals, these languages are not what we converse and write in today. Some form of English is. The study of the great works of English, not to speak of American, literature will remain fundamental, for its models of good writing, if for no other reason.

The worst catastrophe that could befall the study of English literature would be to allow the programs in expository writing to become separate empires in the universities and colleges, wholly cut off from the departments of English and American literature. That this would be a catastrophe for the professors of literature there can be no doubt. Deans, provosts, and presidents these days are a little dubious about the function of the study of literature. In fact many of them have always been dubious. They have tended to assume that the real function of departments of English is to teach good writing. Good writing they understand, or think they do, and are willing to fund. They are much less willing to fund the study of literature, particularly if the enrollments in courses in Chaucer, Milton, and Wordsworth go down markedly. Departments of English that cut themselves off from expository writing will, one can predict, be punished for it. They will atrophy in the way we fear. My ears still ring with the heartfelt exclamation I heard a vice-chancellor at a distinguished state university make in response to a department of literature he thought was not shouldering the burden of expository writing: "I'll starve 'em out!"

On the other side, I am persuaded that programs in expository writing stand to lose much if they are cut off from departments of English literature. This belief rests on a simple premise. Learning to write well cannot be separated from learning to read well. The good departments of English literature have never had as their central mission anything other than teaching how to read well. All the "theory," all the facts of literary history, all the establishing of texts, and so on, have always been ancillary.

I do not minimize the difficulties involved in keeping expository writing and the study of literature together. Nor do I minimize the changes that will be necessary in the present structure of programs in literature, from basic courses for freshmen and sophomores on through the most advanced graduate seminars. I view the development of integrated programs in reading well and in writing well as the major challenge to our profession at the present time.

"Rhetorical study" is the key to this integration. I have the impression that much more has been done already on the side of expository writing than on the side of the study of reading or interpretation. The teaching of writing and reading in high schools, like the teaching of foreign languages, has, I believe, improved in the last decades more than one may think and more than the statistics may yet show. It seems likely to improve even more. Gradually, students will come to college better able to read and write than they have been in the past. Meanwhile, under the pressure of immediate practical need, a large number of teachers all over the country are working out programs in expository writing for this or that college or university. These programs will no doubt gradually be refined until they more or less work, though one should not underestimate the number of failures and inadequacies, many of them almost certainly due at least in part to the unwillingness of legislators, trustees, and administrators to believe how much it costs to do a good job of teaching writing. There will always also be the attempt to fund expository writing at the expense of programs of literature. At the same time, a large and valuable literature on expository writing is developing—not only textbooks of all kinds but an impressive body of theoretical, empirical, and statistical work. Part of the strength of this work is that its authors have, far more than many teachers of literature, quietly accepted and assimilated that transformation in the state of the discipline which I described above. That transformation, of course, has been motivated in good measure by developments in modern linguistics. I am thinking, for example, of what is sometimes called the "paradigm shift" from a referential or mimetic view of language to an active or performative one. People involved at the frontier of this exciting new branch of the broader discipline of English language and literature have the air of persons doing something justifiable and good, while teachers of literature sometimes seem to me to have a furtive and guilty air, as though they were doing something not altogether justifiable in the present context.

It remains for the teachers of literature to catch up and to regain their own sense of frontier excitement. My instincts are strongly preservative or conservative. Nevertheless, I do not believe that an appeal for maintaining traditional humanistic values as a defense of the status quo in literature programs washes well these days, either with students or with the holders of the purse strings, the deans and provosts. I am not at all sure those who go on affirming these pieties believe in them any longer in the old way; sometimes the affirmations sound a bit defensive. Do not misunderstand me. I agree that the study of literature should focus on an exploration of those values. Moral, metaphysical, and religious questions remain the most important ones, in literature as in life, and one of the best places in which to gain an understanding of them is in the masterworks in one's native tongue. The affirmation of humanistic values, however, needs to be accompanied, in the teaching of literature at any rate, by an adequate reading of those texts. Moreover, any defense of literature on the basis of its affirmation of values must be combined these days, I am convinced, with the defense that says one cannot write well, even write well a business letter or a scientific report, unless one can read well the best that has been thought and said in our language.

I have said that the key to the integration of reading and writing is "rhetorical study." Rhetoric has been a two-branched discipline ever since the Greeks. On the one hand, it is the study of persuasion, of how to do things with words. On the other hand, it is the study of the way language works. In particular, it is the study of the function of tropes, the whole panoply of figures, not just metaphor, but metonymy, synecdoche, irony, metalepsis, prosopopoeia, catachresis—the works. It would oversimplify to say that the study of rhetoric as persuasion belongs to expository writing while the study of figurative language belongs to programs in literature. Nevertheless, the relative emphases go in those directions. What is the teaching of writing but the teaching of how to do things with words? This is particularly true for those teachers for whom the paradigm shift from a mimetic to a performative view of language has occurred. What is the teaching of reading but the teaching of the interpretation of tropes? I suspect, however, that the theory and practice of the teaching of expository writing—as sophisticated as they are—are still inhabited and inhibited to some degree by the mirage of straightforward referential language. Good writing, it is still often thought, is calling a spade a spade. On the one hand, such teaching might still have something to learn from those recent developments in literary study that are focused on the problems of figurative language. On the other hand, it is by no means fully accepted by all teachers of literature that the center of our discipline is the teaching of reading and that the center of that is expertise in handling figurative language. Moreover, the question of the performative or persuasive power of language has had an increasing role recently in new theories of reading—for example, in reader-response criticism. Even so, a recognition that all language, even language that seems purely referential or conceptual, is figurative language and an exploration of the consequences of that view for the interpretation of literature represent, it seems to me, one of the major frontiers of literary study today. Most of the new forms of criticism I named earlier—semiotic, Structuralist, Lacanian—not only depend in one way or another on recent theories of language but also recognize in one way or another that the center of literary interpretation is the study of tropes.

Among these kinds of criticism, the form called "deconstruction"—for example, the work of Jacques Derrida and Paul de Man—has especially concerned itself with questions about figurative language. "Deconstruction" is not, as it is sometimes said to be, nihilism or the denial of meaning in literary texts. It is, on the contrary, an attempt to interpret as exactly as possible the oscillations in meaning produced by the irreducibly figurative nature of language. One of the attractions, for me, of such criticism at the present time is that it promises that integration of expository writing and the study of literature which

I believe is the main task facing our profession at the moment. To speak from my own limited experience, such programs as the Literature Major at Yale, and such courses as "Daily Themes," resurrected at Yale by John Hollander, are beginning to make a concentrated effort to develop elaborated curricula combining rhetoric in its two senses. In the fall of 1979 Seabury Press published *Deconstruction and Criticism,* a book by a group of teachers at Yale that attempted to indicate and exemplify, with special reference to Shelley, the direction these new modes of interpreting literature might take. At many of the colleges and universities where I have lectured, I have found young teachers who have been deeply influenced by this form of criticism. Such teachers are beginning in a thoughtful way to work out its consequences for the organization of courses and curricula in English literature.

That the consequences could be substantial changes in the current organization of programs in literature there can be no doubt. I shall conclude this paper by trying to indicate two of these consequences, one affecting our sense of the organization of literature into periods, the other indicating the need for a definition of genres by function rather than by form. My analysis is also meant to exemplify the form of criticism I have just been talking about, as it might be applied not to works of literature themselves but to the conceptualizations by which they have been traditionally organized.

One day he showed me, in confidence and out of vainglory, the cabinet where he kept his letters from women. It was a tall piece of furniture, impressive beneath its bronze appliqués, and was provided with a hundred little drawers.

"Only a hundred!" I exclaimed.

"The drawers are subdivided inside," Damien replied, with the solemnity that never left him.[2]

[Mr. Brooke:] "But now, how do you arrange your documents?"

"In pigeon-holes partly," said Mr. Casaubon, with rather a startled air of effort.

2. Colette, *The Pure and the Impure,* trans. Herma Briffault (New York: Farrar, Straus, 1967), p. 42.

"Ah, pigeon-holes will not do. I have tried pigeon-holes, but every-thing gets mixed in pigeon-holes. I never know whether a paper is in A or Z."[3]

The word "periodization" suggests an act: the act of dividing literary history into segments, or framing it or pigeonholing it, so to speak. We write of medieval literature, the neoclassical period, the baroque, the eighteenth century, Romanticism, the Victorian period, the Pre-Raphaelites, the late Victorians, Modernism, Post-Modernism, and so forth. By what right, according to what measure, guided or supported by what reason, is this framing performed? What justifies it, as one justifies a line of type, rules it, and keeps it from straggling all down the page? Is periodization a free positing or the referential recording of a knowledge? Is it a performative *Setzen,* which makes what it names, or is it a scientific *Erkennen,* which names what is already there? Is it an invocation, an injunction ("Let the Victorian period be!"), or a neutral description ("The Victorian period is")?

The problematic of periodization, it is easy to see, is a par-ticularly complex form of the problematic of naming, as when parents or church or civil authorities name a baby, or when the corpus of an author's work is labeled with the name of the supposed author ("I am reading Shelley"), or when a text is given a title by the author or by others, perhaps by his survivors ("The Triumph of Life"). The complexity in regard to period names lies partly in the evident heterogeneity of the "facts" supposed to be gathered under the single name. How can "Vic-torian literature" label a unity in the same way that the word "Tennyson" presumably does, or "Ulysses"? My last example, however, is already a pun. Do I mean Tennyson's poem or Joyce's novel? Should I have italicized the word instead of put-ting quotation marks around it? How can two works, each with its own self-enclosed uniqueness, have the same title? Does the chronologically later title necessarily allude to the earlier, quote it? The problem here is the reverse of that of twins. If twins are indeed "identical," doubles, should they not have the same

3. George Eliot, *Middlemarch,* (New York: Norton, 1977), bk. I, ch. ii.

name, not Shem and Shaun or Jacob and Esau, but Shem One and Shem Two, Esau and Esau, or Jacob and Jacob?

The special complexity of period naming enters by way of the necessary incorporation into its problematic of all the issues involving history and literary history. Does literary history exist, in the sense of an orderly narrative and causal sequence, readable, comprehensible by the imaginative reason? Or is it no more than a vast shifting fabrication, made up after the fact by the historians? If literary history exists, is the specificity of a literary period some self-enclosed uniqueness, or perhaps imposed from outside time by occult spiritual forces? Or is it the result of an orderly and inevitable development from the period before, determined by its predecessor, forecast perhaps by some predictable negative reaction, the son killing the father but even in doing so being ruled by him, Romanticism following Neoclassicism, the post-Modern the Modern, as the night the day, or day night? Is it, as my last figure suggests, and as some historians have argued, a matter of natural rhythms? Are literary periods part of nature, like the circuits of the sun and the moon, the turn of the seasons, the rise and fall of the tides? Such a view might justify all our habitual metaphors of genesis, growth, and development from period to period in literary history. Or is the specificity of each period a matter of a particular social structure, a particular assemblage of material means of communication, production, distribution, and consumption? Is Victorian literature a result of the railroad and the proliferation of printed periodicals, or, to put the question another way, is it a result of the absence of television?

The problem of period names, in short, is metaphysical through and through, for periodization involves the whole network of assumptions about beginning, causality, end, and ground that makes up the fabric of Occidental metaphysics, that fabric which has bound together Western culture since Plato's precursors and the Old Testament prophets, our bifurcated heterogeneous "genesis." To put the validity of period names in question is therefore an intrinsic part of what is sometimes today called "The deconstruction of metaphysics," though such putting in question has of course always been a part of metaphysics, as a parasite within the host. Deconstruction is not itself period-bound. It is part of any period in our history.

The problematic of period names includes the following issues, among others: Who has the right to name the period? Must a genuine period name be given by those living within the period, or can a period be recognized and named only after the fact. Is the name, in other words, inside or outside the borders of the period itself? This question, as can be seen, is a version of the question whether the title of a work of literature is part of the work or affixed from the outside as an arbitrary and perhaps falsifying label. Does the name of a period indicate its intrinsic essence, its very being, or is it a convenient fiction? Is "P. B. Shelley" really "P. B. Shelley," or has someone exercised his or her will to power over him by giving him a name foreign to what he really is? If its very being is the source of a given period label, is that label grounded in some transcendent or supernatural power that orders history and literary history, or is it immanent within history itself?

It is easy enough to claim to reject both of these last alternatives as obfuscations, one form or another of the mystification of the zeitgeist, though I believe some implicit or unthought-through acceptance of one or the other is more deeply ingrained than one might think. It is also easier to dismiss the dialectical-material, natural, and history-of-ideas explanations than really to free oneself of their assumptions. Even if one accepts the notion that period names are fictions through and through, baseless performatives, one would need to explain their complex function in the institutionalized study of literature—for example, in American colleges and universities. That function has to do with matters of political, academic, and spiritual "power," if there is such a thing. It has to do with the organization of courses, curricula, programs, catalogs, the placement of books in libraries, scholarly and critical journals, professional organizations and meetings, the structure of ranks within departments of English, French, German, and so forth, the making and not making of academic careers. Someone invents the term "Post-Modernism," and behold! a new discipline springs up, with journals, courses, jostlings for prestige, and so on. The pigeonholing by periods, moreover, differs more than one might at first think from department to department within the same university, from university to university, college to college, and from country to country in the West. "Modern English Literature" at the University of Zurich, for example, is everything after Shakespeare, whereas "Modernism" at Yale begins about 1890, as far as I can tell. Period terms are translatable from one Occidental language and institution to another, but not wholly so. They are both translatable and untranslatable, like any terms that one tries to move from one "natural language" to another.

One way to see the complexities of what might be meant by calling period names fictions is to observe that they are all figures of speech. They are therefore open to tropological analysis. An amazing potpourri of forms of figuration, in fact, is to be found in the period names we have. All are to be placed somewhere on the metaphor-synecdoche-metonymy axis, but just where would lead in each case to a different set of implications. Every period name is in one way or another a synecdoche, a part taken as representative of the whole. The question is whether the chosen part is genuinely similar to the whole, metaphorically valid, or whether it is a mere contingent metonymy, a piece of a heterogeneous mixture chosen arbitrarily to stand for the whole or to make a mélange without intrinsic unity seem like a whole.

Each period name begs innumerable questions about the nature of the period. Each is a strategic interpretation, for "political" purposes, according to one or another mode of figurative reduction. The incoherence of period names is striking, and to unfold the implications of any one would demand a long analysis. The analysis would tend to dissolve the unity and historical uniqueness of the period in question, as A. O. Lovejoy's celebrated analyses of Romanticism reduce it to a heterogeneous collection of "romanticisms," or as Paul de Man's discussion of "Modernism" shows it to be a concept by no means unique to a single period but a recurrent ever-repeated self-subverting move in each period's sense of itself in relation to previous periods. If de Man is right the term "Post-Modern" is a tautology or an oxymoron, since no writer or critic ever reaches the modern, in the sense of the authentically self-born, much less goes beyond it. The "modern" is the always-ready and the always not-yet of periodization.

I have said that each period term demands a long analysis, but in a moment one can see that several ("Renaissance," "Neoclassicism," "Pre-Raphaelitism") involve the notion of repetition. In each of these the specificity of the period defines itself or is defined as the recurrence, whether genuine or in parody, of an earlier period. The word "classicism" itself implies classification or pigeonholing, that affirmation of male mastery over the muse of history in all her elusive documentary incarnations. Some period names seem scrupulously neutral or merely chronological ("the eighteenth century"), but chronological classification is of course once more a metaphysical notion, calling up inevitably ideas of historical causation. Other period terms describe in figure a stylistic feature ("the baroque"). Both "the baroque" and "the Renaissance" imply an assimilation of the period to nature. The baroque is rough, like an irregular pearl, and in the Renaissance the classical world was self-born, born anew. Other period names label the period metonymically with the name of its monarch ("Victorian," "Edwardian"). Others ("Romanticism," "Modernism") involve a complex interpretation of previous periods, as well as a double contradictory claim that the period in question is unique and novel and that the quality in question is universal and recurrent. The coming to consciousness of literature as literature in the German Romantics, especially in Friedrich Schlegel, is exemplary here, as Phillipe Lacoue-Labarthe and Jean-Luc Nancy have admirably argued.[4]

As an example of the way a period name is an archival function, a necessary hypothetical fiction, and a strategic performative, operating inside the body of literature it labels but at the same time imposed from the outside and maintained for some purposeful taking possession, I shall, in conclusion, discuss

4. Phillipe Lacoue-Labarthe and Jean-Luc Nancy, *L'Absolu littéraire: Théorie de la littérature du romantisme allemand* (Paris: Seuil, 1978).

briefly the term "Victorian fiction." According to one pigeon-holing, the term "Victorian fiction" is a subtitle within the larger title "realistic fiction"; according to another it is a subdivision of "the Victorian period."

"Realistic fiction" has as perhaps its most salient characteristic the ability to create the powerful phantasms of personalities. The reader feels he knows Elizabeth Bennett, Dorothea Brooke, Plantagenet Palliser, Michael Henchard, and Joe Christmas in the same way he knows his friends or relatives. Perhaps he knows them even better. One of the powerful attractions of reading novels (when this activity was a central feature of our culture, as it probably no longer is) was the way they seemed to give an even more intimate access to the mind and heart of another person than the reader could ever feel himself to have in "real life." Nevertheless, the feeling that one is encountering a "character," a "person," "another self" is demonstrably an illusion, both in the novel and in real life. It is as much an illusion as the other basic concepts of Occidental metaphysics, with which it is inextricably connected. Moreover, if the realistic novels of the last four hundred years have strongly reinforced the illusion of selfhood, they have at the same time constantly and explicitly deconstructed that illusion. They have shown it to be the result of a misinterpretation, the misreading of signs.

There is no "real novel," however, from *Don Quixote* to *Ulysses, The Waves,* or even *L'Innomable,* that does not create in two ways the powerful illusion of characters. One is the illusion of the character of the narrator. The narrator seems to be a man (or woman) speaking to us. There is an almost irresistible temptation to think of the narrative voice as that of the author. The second illusion is that of the characters in the story. They seem to be men and women like ourselves. This positing of two forms of character is a distinguishing feature of novels as such, or perhaps of narrative as such, since who would deny these illusions, *mutatis mutandis,* to fairy tales, to Norse sagas, or the *The Odyssey?*

The function of novels within the community of their readers may by hypothesis be said to be circular. Each culture, as well as each period of that culture, has its own complex presuppositions about selfhood. An example would be the relatively fixed notion of selfhood in England, perhaps reinforced by certain aspects of Protestantism, as against the relatively fluid feeling for character in France. Novels reinforce and partly create these presuppositions in each community of readers—or did during the period the novel reigned as a major genre. Readers go to a novel to be reassured, to encounter characters "like themselves." They read the novel according to their presuppositions about selfhood, so that, confronted by the characters on the page that have the magic power to generate the illusion of character, they are like a child with a hobbyhorse, not like the "savage" at the cinema. Once that interpretation has been made, however, once they have yielded to the illusion of knowing Pip, Lord Jim, Elizabeth Bennett, or Dorothea Brooke, following their lives through as they follow the text through, knowing them better and better, knowing them intimately from within, they turn the line around and interpret their neighbors and themselves according to the models they have encountered in novels. They people the world with Willoughbys, Claras, and Dorotheas. In this way nature imitates art. England after 1836 begins to be filled with Dickensian characters, even with people who feel themselves to be Dickensian characters.

The novel, then, has had a powerful, perhaps indispensable, social function during its reign. The fictions of character and the characteristic life lines of characters that it sustains and creates have formed one of the fundamental cohesive forces keeping each community of readers together. A community may be defined as a group of people who live by the same fictions, the same simplifications, the same hypostatized figures posited as substances. The novel has helped to make and maintain such communities.

This function of the novel seems clear enough, but what is the function of the contrary aspect of each work of fiction, its putting in question of the notions of character from which it derives its benign power to buttress society? This disintegrating would seem to be not only antisocial but even auto-destructive, since it demolishes the illusion of character on which the novel's power and function depend. This autodeconstruction reduced the readers of a given novel to the state of children who have outgrown their toys and see the sticks and yarn behind the hobbyhorse. Why is this dissolution of its own fundamental fiction as constant a feature of realistic fiction as the creation of the fiction of character in the first place?

I suggest that the function is apotropaic. It is a throwing away of what is already thrown away, in order to save it. It is a destroying of the already destroyed, in order to preserve the illusion that it is still intact. All men and women living within a culture accepting a certain notion of character have an uneasy feeling that their belief in character, even their belief in their own characters, may be confidence in an illusion. The function of the self-deconstructive aspect of novels would then be to assuage this covert suspicion by expressing it overtly, in a safe region of fiction. Character is thus triumphantly reaffirmed in the face of its being put in question, even if that reaffirmation may be no more than the persistence of that deconstructing voice, the voice of the narrator who says "I am I," and who goes on saying "I am I" even when he has demonstrated that there is no "I," or the persistence of the character who says, "I have and am no I."

My hypothesis, then: the novel as the perpetual tying and untying of the knot of selfhood works, in the psychic economy of the individual and of the community, to affirm the fiction of character by putting it fictionally in question and thus short-circuits a doubt that, left free to act in the real social world, might destroy both self and community. Belief in the subject, in character, is thereby precariously maintained by the novel over the abyss of its dismantling. Is not the positing of the subject necessary to the positing of its fictionality, in a perpetual torsion of nay saying and yea saying, of nay saying that cannot be said without the yea saying its saying unsays? The novel demonstrates, in a "safe" realm where nothing serious is at stake, the possibility of maintaining the fiction of selfhood in the teeth of a recognition that selfhood is a fictive projection, an "interpretation" not a fact, and is always open to being dissolved by a contrary interpretation—for example, that of the multiplicity or the nonentity of the ego. The novel is an instrument, a production of its society that has a certain function within the psychic economy of that society. It is not a mimetic copy of something that could do perfectly well without the copy.

Nor is it the creation of a supplementary alternative "world" with no relation, other than that of accurate mirroring, to the real social world.

The same linguistic materials—or their approximate translations from country to country, language to language, dialect to dialect, century to century—have always been available within the Occident, since its "dawn," to use another familiar figure from nature. In a period of less than three thousand years there have not been enough changes in our Western languages or even enough changes in our means of production, consumption, and living together to make the sequence of periods more than a series of permutations of the same materials. The specificity of a period lies in the special way these materials are put together at a given time and in a given place, for example in Victorian England. It lies also in the special function these materials so selectively organized have in that particular country and time, or within a particular class in that country. I have taken as my example "Victorian fiction." There is nothing in that whole body of novels in the way of technique, conventions, themes, assumptions about character, society, and so on that is unique to the period. All have clear parallels earlier and later. Nevertheless, Victorian fiction is different in the proportion of the mixture, so to speak, and in the function that the novels as physical objects, works printed in book or periodical form, had in the culture for which they were produced.

It is therefore legitimate to speak of "the Victorian novel" or even of "the Victorian period." Yes, Virginia, there is a Victorian period. It has the same kind of existence as does Santa Claus. The Victorian period is the result of many performative acts of language bringing together a fiction that exists, but never as present or as presence. If this is so, this fact should have certain consequences for the organization of departments, courses, curricula, careers, for all those pigeonholings, runnings, and followings of paths that make up the phantasmal mappings and boundaries by which the study of literature is institutionalized.

Not least of these mappings would be a result of the recognition that the function of Victorian novels for the Victorians and their function for us should not be assumed to be the same. In that effort of integrating programs in reading and in writing

I have been advocating here the central question would be not "What function did these Victorian novels have for the Victorians" but "What is the function, the efficacy, of Victorian novels here and now, in this particular context?" That there is still a function it has been the whole purpose of this essay to argue.

If my discussion of the figures or periodization and of the performative function of Victorian novels exemplifies the two branches of rhetoric described earlier, it hardly constitutes a detailed plan for those curricular changes in the study of literature I think necessary. These should in any case occur gradually from within. The traditional historical organization by periods and genres should be dismantled only when we are sure we have alternatives that will be better. Much is gained, even for creative teaching, by having a firm rubric like "Victorian fiction" within which to teach, rather than having to invent the whole syllabus from the ground up every time one presents a course. It is also true, however, that the rubrics may no longer fit in the contexts in which the teaching of literature functions or correspond to the teacher's insights into how reading should be taught. In such circumstances, the old rubrics should probably go.

The exact form the new courses and curricula will take is hard to predict, but there will undoubtedly be some breaking down of the old pigeonholing by periods and genres, more attention to the problems of interpreting nonfictional prose (philosophical and critical texts) along with plays, novels, and poems. There will also probably be a recognition that the problems of interpretation—for example, the decisive function of figurative language in making meaning heterogeneous or undecidable—cut across period lines and generic lines. The methods used to read a passage by Locke, or an essay by Kenneth Burke or William Empson, must be similar to those used to read Shelley or Dickens. The newly organized courses are likely to find it necessary to include texts in other languages, probably to be read in translation, at least in the undergraduate curriculum. It will be necessary to pay some attention to the original languages, however, and to the problems of translation. If Montaigne, Rousseau, Diderot, Goethe, Kleist, or Nietzsche are to be taught, the inadequacies of any translations must somehow be confronted in the teaching. Such new courses will probably best be developed by young teachers who have been influenced by the new modes of thinking in expository writing and in the interpretation of literature. It is these teachers who must respond to the immediate needs of their students and of the institutions where they teach. Some utopian planning and theorizing, however, may also be helpful. Though many articles, essays, and even books applying the new modes of criticism to English and American texts already exist, the new teaching of literature does not yet have its *Understanding Poetry* or its version of the Norton *Anthology*. These would be textbooks trying to work out the practical consequences for introductory courses of assuming that a good work of literature may be a heterogeneous assemblage rather than an "organic unity," that the key to understanding it is a sophistication in the interpretation of figures, and that its function may be more performative than mimetic. A period of rapid change in a discipline has its excitements and challenges. Of these we may expect to have plenty in the next decades.

DAVID PERKINS

Taking Stock After Thirty Years

I used to think that the literature we taught was itself the teacher. The nominal teacher in the classroom performed a useful role if he or she enhanced the impact of the texts, something my teachers did not always do. To teach literature was different from teaching, say, economics, since as an object of knowledge the economy was not also, like literature, valuable experience in itself. Rather, the aim of an economics teacher was to convey ideas and methods by which the economy might be understood and even regulated. For this reason I disliked Northrop Frye's dictum, in *Anatomy of Criticism,* that one teaches not literature but criticism. It made the teaching of literature analogous to disciplines such as economics, for it substituted, as the subject matter, the concepts of a learned profession for literature itself. If Frye's criticism were the example, a teacher would expound theories about fictional modes, archetypes, genres, and their interrelations. Teachers from other critical schools would present different items—the use of the persona in satiric poetry, the distinction between plot *(siuzhet)* and story *(fabula)* in narrative—but from my point of view the procedure would be the same: critical concepts would be the subject of instruction, and texts would be discussed primarily as illustration. Such teaching would illuminate some aspects of texts at the expense

111

of their totality, though, inconsistently, a more refined experience of the totality would be put forward as the justification. Metacriticism involved a further recession from literature, since the criticism of criticism seldom enriched the experience of texts, at least not directly.

I also rejected another principle of Northrop Frye's, that the forms and conventions of literature come only from previous literature. Texts, in my opinion, also reflected both the personality and experience of the author and the historical life of his or her society, and not only in their contents but also in their forms. And they articulated or implied *Weltanschauungen*—"visions of life," "orderings of experience"—which had been held by historical persons and cultures. Moreover, readers always implicitly compared and related the life presented in literature to their own, thus perceiving themselves and their lives more clearly. Otherwise, their reading would be merely vicarious and aesthetic, which was impossible and, if possible, grossly impoverished. The interconnections of literature and life must be a subject of teaching because in them literature had its largest interest and significance. We must allow the text to "encounter" us, as Gadamer would put it, activating and addressing our vital concerns, as the archaic torso of Apollo, in Rilke's poem, observed the observer and demanded that he change: "Du musst dein Leben ändern."

The purpose of this essay is to ask myself to what extent I still hold these beliefs. But first I must mention a point in which my practice was inconsistent with my ideas. I would as a teacher discuss the text in relation to biographical and historical reality in the past, and also as a "vision of life," but I was very unwilling to extend discussion of its reception to myself. To present literature impersonally and objectively was a cardinal point of classroom morality. In this I was typical of most university teachers of literature of my generation, and the prestige of science is usually cited as an explanation for the sought-after objectivity. But I was not emulating science. I was transposing into teaching and criticism some ideals of the *fin de siècle,* which I caught from T. S. Eliot and, in lesser degree, from the New Critics. They conveyed that the personal is not worth expressing, that a teacher must suppress the self, which is "worthless," as Eliot said, and concentrate on the object. As the ideals of the 1890s were reflected in the teaching of the 1950s, the teacher-critic corresponded to the poet, and literature, the text, to that "beauty" which the ninetyish poet contemplated and sought to render, forgetting himself in devotion to it. In the particular version of this structure caught from Eliot, the teacher-critic was analogous to the impersonal poet. The reactions which took place in his mind were somehow not his own. The object of his attention was the text, or possibly the author, but it was also the process of reacting itself, for there was a self-conscious concern that this should be as accurate, refined, precise, and complete as possible. That the university teaching of literature—with its close readings, its interpretations seemingly derived from the text and not also from the reader, its low-keyed terms, and its pursuit of formal problems—reflected a past phase of literature is not in the least atypical, for in relation to developments in literature, English departments are always provincial. The way I taught literature must have modified the way I read it, but obviously, under this system of inhibitions, there was still a considerable discrepancy between my actual responses and concerns in reading and what I discussed in class. Since this division was largely the result of a particular system of ideas, it could be overcome when the ideas were rejected. Of course I am not now advocating an *étalage du moi,* confessional and monologic, in the classroom. I am merely saying that since all reading and understanding are inevitably personal, it is phony to pretend otherwise. In fact, a personal interpretation claims less authority and promotes dialogue better than an impersonal one that is supposedly stamped by the text on everyone who reads it carefully.

So far as I now question the beliefs sketched in the two opening paragraphs, the cause does not lie in arguments against them. Arguments can always be met with counterarguments and are seldom decisive in questions of belief. The changes, which it would be banal to cite, in students and in the historical setting are of course important factors, but not, I think, the primary ones. The most troubling problem is the collision between my former ideas about teaching and the values and institutional requirements of the rest of professional life. In relation to literature we function in three different ways, as readers, teachers, and critics or researchers aiming to publish. While we are actually reading literature, we more or less forget our research preoccupations. Deconstructive critics ignore the indeterminacy of meanings, literary historians put aside "influences," and both, like ordinary readers, become absorbed in the plot, characters, and imaginative effects, being caught up in the work totally. The experience is emotive, personal, and enormously ramified. To express it in teaching is to some degree possible, as I said, but it can hardly be expressed at all in published research and criticism with its specialized topics. The relations of research to teaching are a more difficult issue.

By my principles they could not be united, for, to repeat, if we taught our critical ideas or research we would develop only limited aspects of the textual whole, and we would, in most cases, inhibit the experience of "encounter." Yet not to integrate them is impossible for both intellectual and practical reasons. To teach in one compartment and do research in another is unsatisfactory, for we are then committed to two different sets of values and methods, and ourselves become compartmentalized. Moreover, methods of teaching which may correspond to the experience of reading but not to specialized research leave one intellectually dissatisfied. Everyone has had such teaching, and there are innumerable written models of its procedures. Their genre is commentary—for example, the early books of Harold Bloom on Shelley, Blake, Yeats, and *The Visionary Company*. That the commentary starts from and remains focused on the text and that it openly engages personal responses and vital concerns are strengths. But its unsystematic, eclectic procedures make it harder to pursue an argument in detail and generally do not promote intellectual depth, rigor, edge, and coherence, however brilliant the *obiter dicta*.

Meanwhile, the profession reserves its rewards overwhelmingly for research and publication, so that time spent on teaching actually hinders one's career. There is hardly a university in the country where reputation, promotion, and salary do not depend primarily or exclusively on publications and on other activities related to research, such as getting grants and speaking at conferences. That, nevertheless, so much time and effort is put into teaching tells a great deal about the real motives of the people entering the profession, and about what they experience as pleasurable in their work. It further suggests that the pressure to publish comes more from administrators than from faculty, which would, if left to itself, have a somewhat different system of values. Be this as it may, the institutional overestimation of research means, inevitably, that research interests must be incorporated with teaching. I wish I had a dollar for every time a dean or well-meaning colleague has told me that teaching and research nourish each other. The truth is that as the profession is set up, teaching must be subordinated to research, and we teach the theses and books we have already written, or we teach the topics that will lead to new articles and books. Nor is this done in a cynical spirit. With so much time, energy, competitiveness, and career invested in them, the subjects of our research naturally also become our consuming intellectual interests, and we endow them with a greater importance than, in a more objective view, they may merit. As we teach them, therefore, we feel that we are presenting concepts of intense fascination and significance, as indeed, in many cases, we are, and our enthusiasm for our subjects makes us good teachers. There is, then, nothing wrong in itself and much that is right, as well as inevitable, about making our research the subject of our teaching. It is wrong only because it displaces a better subject and aim.

What happens when a text "encounters" us? According to Gadamer, such an encounter is always primarily with meaning, and with a meaning that "really concerns us," as though the text "addressed and intended us." In contrast, a merely aesthetic experience of the text deprives it of its full being. It strips the text of its social purposes or functions and of its bearing and impact on moral and religious beliefs. A merely aesthetic awareness of a text cannot even influence our attitudes to whatever the text is itself all about. With respect to a historical reading of texts the argument is more complicated. At one extreme, to seek to reconstruct the meaning of the text for its original author and audience would be restrictive. Such a meaning would be an abstraction, something we can try to describe but never actually experience, for the full present being of the text includes all its previous reception and interpretation so far as they now modify our perception of it. At the other extreme, merely to project our own preoccupations into the text is impossible and, if possible, would be of little value.

Nevertheless, reading becomes an "encounter" because it involves interpreting, and in the process of interpreting we find our own preoccupations addressed within the text. We are not passive in this process, for we read the text with a selective foregrounding of our own concerns and even make it address questions that were not present to its author. Yet we do not, to repeat, interpret with subjective automatism, in blindness to the text, but respond to a potentiality of meaning that the text actually contains. It is quite possible, for example, that Shakespeare never consciously conceived the sympathetic interpretations of Shylock that have been common since the 1890s. But he wrote the words that permit these interpretations, and the reason he wrote these words is ultimately the same as the reason we interpret them as we do. Both we and Shakespeare share the same broad tradition of Western values and of assumptions about a universal human nature; his plays contribute to this tradition and thus help further to form us in such a way that we understand Shakespeare and legitimately extend the meanings of his texts through our own interpretations. To put it another way, our interpretations are determined by our expectation of truth; we anticipate that the text will say what we hold to be true, and try to interpret it so that it does. In fact, Gadamer remarks, "Only when the attempt to accept what is said as true fails, do we try to 'understand' the text, psychologically or historically, as another's meaning." An encounter, then, presupposes that we share with a text a sufficient common ground of perceptions, assumptions, and values, that there is a "fusion of horizons" such that we can be involved with its meaning, and the encounter takes place when we interpret a text so that it speaks to our deepest concerns. The creativity of the encounter, Gadamer adds, may even go further. Sometimes it is "as in true conversation, where also something comes out that neither of the partners contains in himself."[1]

---

1. Hans-Georg Gadamer, *Wahrheit und Methode,* 5th ed., in *Gesammelte Werke* (Tübingen: J. C. B. Mohr, 1986), I, pp. 465–466, 299, 466.

The interrelation of our reading, teaching, and writing is a problem to which there is no satisfactory solution. Nevertheless, we should seek to heighten our awareness of it, hoping that the tension and self-criticism generated by this awareness may be productive. Our experience as readers should create dissatisfaction with our teaching and writing, and as writers with our teaching. Ideally our teaching would have something of the method, sophistication, rigor, and detail of our specialized research, and our writing would engage our existential concerns. Our reading would be an "encounter," and the expression of this would also be central both to our teaching and writing. Like all ideal demands, these cannot be fully realized in practice, but neither can they be surrendered.

Practices and Theories

ROBERT N. WATSON

Teaching "Shakespeare": Theory versus Practice

"Practically"—he felt himself getting the last of his chance—"there is *no author; that is for us to deal with. There are all the immortal people—in the work; but there's nobody else."*

"Yes," said the young man—"that's what it comes to. There should really, to clear the matter up, be no such Person."

"As you say," Gedge returned, "it's what it comes to. There is *no such Person."*

The evening air listened, in the warm thick midland stillness, while the wife's little cry rang out. "But wasn't *there—?"*

    —Henry James, "The Birthplace"

A taboo has developed in recent years against considering Shakespeare as a person rather than as a textual entity. Scholars are trained to acknowledge a virtually complete schism between the man and the works, with neither one capable of affecting or revealing the other in any valid way. One of the few things New Critics, Marxists, and deconstructionists agree on is the essential irrelevance of the author. Nonetheless, most of us still teach literature in a way that depends on the idea of a historical author. Our reluctance to banish Shakespeare from the classroom entirely seems to me healthy, provided we recognize and understand the discrepancy between our theories as critics and our practices as teachers. If we admit this author-as-oracle too complacently, we risk methodological hypocrisy, indulging our emotions and our egotism at the expense of our intelligence.

121

But if we completely suppress our sense of a person behind the plays, we dehumanize some of the most influential artworks in our culture and waste an extraordinary opportunity to teach something beyond literary technique. Certainly there are problems, both theoretical and practical, with allowing some posited historical/biographical Shakespeare to dominate an undergraduate course. There are also ethical problems with using such a course to teach a particular set of .values under the guise of teaching literary works. But while the unexamined Shakespeare may not be worth teaching, a depersonalized text may be a pointlessly impoverished one.[1] So when I was asked to write about "what is needed now" in the teaching of Shakespeare, the best answer I could find was, Shakespeare himself.

When I tell people that I "teach Shakespeare," I of course do not mean to imply that I teach the man rather than the plays. If challenged, I would probably specify that I teach a body of work. But whose body? What is the significance of that anthropomorphic metaphor? And is it an anatomy class, in which the point is to ignore the unity and humanity of this body, or a love affair, in which those things are (ideally) the main point? Where does a love of Shakespeare cross into the realms of fetishism or idolatry, generating propaganda and precluding effective analysis?

Teaching something called a "Shakespeare course" suggests a belief that there is something unitary to the works, or something that can be productively imagined as unitary. We may, under pressure from the current critical orthodoxy, remark to each other knowingly that there is no such thing as an author

1. C. L. Barber, "Shakespeare in his Sonnets," *Massachusetts Review*, 1 (1959), 649, makes a similar observation on a more particular basis: "It is better to read the sonnets for universal values than to lose their poetry. But to block off consideration of what they mean as an expression of Shakespeare's own experience is a needless sacrifice, which leads in practice to ignoring those many sonnets which hinge on the stresses of the poet's personal life, and to losing an important part of the meaning and beauty of the whole collection."

in the text.[2] But most Shakespeareans still commonly choose to teach the plays in the supposed order of their composition, and to teach, say, *The Comedy of Errors* and *The Merry Wives of Windsor* instead of an arguably better comedy such as Jonson's *The Alchemist,* or even a comedy arguably more Shakespearean in its theme such as Nashe's *Summer's Last Will and Testament.* The canon we teach, then, whether out of habit or conviction, is based on a notion of authorial identity rather than strictly on literary qualities.

Few modern Shakespeareans would dare say explicitly that our courses will teach "what Shakespeare had to say about life," but most of us (by my observation) teach the same thing implicitly. If one accepts the Romantic view of literature as "the record of the best and happiest moments of the happiest and best minds,"[3] it is natural to want to transcribe that record for ourselves and our students, in hopes of reconstructing such ideal mental moments for our own use. When we say we are "reading Shakespeare," the casual shorthand may be revealing: we are trying to decipher not just a series of words, but also an intelligence, its experience and insights. All our efforts to isolate the real intentions of the author, or (to replace those dangerous words with slightly less dangerous ones) the central themes and images of the plays, are primarily efforts to identify something within the plays as Shakespeare's own voice. We credit Shakespeare for the magnificent autonomy of his characters, for making them serve his dramatic strategies without depriving them of full and authentic humanity. At the same time, however, we

2. Michel Foucault, "What Is an Author," in *Language, Counter-Memory, Practice,* ed. Donald F. Bouchard; trans. Donald F. Bouchard and Sherry Simon (Ithaca: Cornell University Press, 1977), p. 118, comments that "It has been understood that the task of criticism is not to reestablish the ties between an author and his work or to reconstitute an author's thought and experience through his works." See also the clear and capacious discussion of these issues in Norman Rabkin, *Shakespeare and the Problem of Meaning* (Chicago: University of Chicago Press, 1981).

3. Percy Bysshe Shelley, "A Defence of Poetry," in *The Prose Works of Percy Bysshe Shelley,* ed. Richard Herne Shepherd (London: Chatto and Windus, 1912), II, p. 33.

persist in seeing those characters as pawns in a game of allegorical communication, refracted bits of the authorial vision that
our critical prism can refocus into something recognizable and
"Shakespearean." We seem to believe that there lurks, beneath
the text of each play, a subtext that is more authentic to the
author himself, a palimpsest text that can be rendered legible
by the right angle of view, by some sort of enhanced enlightenment. We may be conscious that our role as interpreters
moves us away from the "erotics" of the text, toward hermeneutics,[4] but it is easy to overlook the fact that we are also being
propelled toward biography, even hagiography.

Many Shakespeare survey courses still begin with some version of the traditional "Shakespeare, Lad of Stratford" lecture.
There are many justifications for that sort of beginning. Since
the students have not yet read any of the plays, there is no
literary text to discuss, and it is tempting to start them off with
something approximately factual—especially when so many of
them seem to be brimful with such vivid and unfactual ideas
about Shakespeare and his world. Such a lecture is also a way
of forestalling what seems to be (at least among academically
unsophisticated students) a primary line of inquiry: did Shakespeare really write Shakespeare? Wry practitioners of theoretical criticism such as Roland Barthes and Stanley Fish would
doubtless savor all the implications of that question, but what
interests me here is how appealing and important the personal
side of our topic is to people who are not Shakespeare specialists. Granted, biography may be inherently more accessible,
or more immediately accessible, than drama. But it should worry
us that, for all our talk about what wondrously interesting and
realistic characters Shakespeare created, our students so often
find it more interesting to speculate about the real person
who created them. Perhaps they are simply missing the point,
but I suspect there is more to it than that. Such students may
also be reading the implicit subtext of our text, recognizing that
(for all our denials) the author is an essential premise of our

---

4. Susan Sontag, "Against Interpretation," rpt. in *Twentieth Century Literary
Criticism,* ed. David Lodge (London: Longman, 1972), pp. 652–660, offers a
polemical definition of this distinction.

lectures, and getting to know him an essential goal of the course.

Shakespeare professors are certainly more self-conscious than they were fifty years ago about filling out the biography with sentimental speculations, and about making the relationship between the biography and the drama a directly causal one. This particular genre of introductory lecture—perhaps a vestige from an earlier phase in the evolution of Shakespeare studies—becomes more sophisticated as we become more defensive about the rationale for teaching a Shakespeare course *per se*. Thus, instead of retelling a deer-poaching anecdote, we might put the eighty-three different Elizabethan spellings of Shakespeare's name up on the board, and make that a kind of deconstructionist lesson in the futility of biographical determinism. If we do relate a few choice anecdotes from Samuel Schoenbaum's *Shakespeare's Lives*,[5] we might use them as a lesson in the way biography is a fiction susceptible to the changing needs and presuppositions of changing historical ideologies.

But diffident, decentering gestures of this sort betoken a resistance to a powerful centripetal force, an attraction toward the notion that there might be a single consciousness at the center of the works we will be teaching. The suggestion lingers in the air, at the end of the introductory hour, that the course might be an attempt to conjure that poor ghost. Even if the text is shattered by deconstruction into something as incoherent as a ouija board, it can still be used for conjuration by a community of believers. Our job description comes to include the role of medium; our success or failure (in the eyes of our colleagues as well as our students) depends on whether we convince them that we are actually in possession of Shakespeare, and speaking in his tongues, or whether we appear instead merely as frauds, and the plays we offer as mere forgeries under Shakespeare's name.

The ending of most Shakespeare lecture courses is no less symptomatic. A professor who finishes by quoting a few lines from Prospero (very likely the Epilogue, in hope of applause)

5. Samuel Schoenbaum, *Shakespeare's Lives* (Oxford: Oxford University Press, 1970).

fulfills the implication that a Shakespeare course is largely a mimesis of the biography, and a conjuration of the deified author's own voice, which finally speaks through the mouth of a high priest. This implication pleases our professorial vanity, and offers a satisfying subliminal symmetry to the experience of the course. It is also delightfully empowering to leave hovering unchallenged in the students' minds the notion of a discernible and moralizing Shakespeare, because that notion allows us to express our opinions on a variety of matters and attribute those opinions to this authoritative figure. Though we are not in a position to claim that what we want is what God or nature dictates (as racists, sexists, and imperialists like to claim), we have something almost as good: we can recommend a philosophy, a theology, or a mode of conduct under the pretext that Shakespeare recommends it.[6]

I don't know how to avoid that practice, or even whether it ought to be avoided. In lecturing on *Measure for Measure,* for example, I describe that play as Shakespeare's argument for a proper balance between indulgence and repression. What I mean is that the action and the verbal peculiarities of the play demonstrate—as if they were designed to advocate—the desirability of such a balance. Behind my lecture is a convenient fiction, whereby I postulate the likeliest series of responses in what I define as an ideal reader, and translate that into an argument by the author. The attribution of the play's effects to Shakespearean intention is then fairly easy, since an argument implies an intention, which implies an intender, a role for which Shakespeare is the likeliest candidate. But one would like to believe that the moral argument of this play (if such it is, if such I can show it to be) can stand on its own, without the sort of *ad*

6. Shakespeare criticism therefore becomes a fiercely partisan contest, even when conducted subtly under the guise of scholarly disinterestedness. A Christian who could demonstrate that the plays are an encoding of Christianity would have won a powerful endorsement for his or her belief. A similar claim on behalf of psychoanalysis could—and, I believe, did and does—greatly broaden the acceptance of that system. Even deconstructionists, paradoxically enough, study the words of this great authority searching for definitive endorsements of deconstruction.

hominem support involved in putting the weight of Shakespeare's own cultural prestige behind it.

Beyond such tendentiousness, however, the sense of an author behind the plays is necessary if we are to retain much of what we value in those plays. What would the "negative capability" that Keats praised in Shakespeare mean,[7] if we did not envision a single personality creating the plays? Surely the appeal of that concept comes from something more than the supposition that the plays leave issues unresolved, teach evenhandedness, and grant equal status to the contradictory worldviews of various characters. No one would attribute the genius of "negative capability" to the transcript of a debate between a liberal and a conservative. What is fascinating is the idea of a single consciousness that has managed to discover and inhabit a distant vantage-point where oppositions that seem to us irreconcilable can be imaginatively conjoined. Both the tragedies and the romances seem more significant, and more consoling, if we can consider the essentially biographical idea that someone who experienced the terrifyingly bleak vision of *King Lear* could recover to write *The Tempest*.[8]

Much of what we teach about Shakespeare's works, and cherish about Shakespeare's works, thus depends on the idea of Shakespeare himself. The theoretical question of whether any authorial presence can survive within a text may be countered with a practical question: can a text survive without a perceived authorial presence, even an anonymous one? If the author is dead, as Michel Foucault and Roland Barthes assert,[9] can the

7. John Keats, *The Letters of John Keats, 1814–1821,* 2 vols., ed. Hyder Rollins (Cambridge, Mass.: Harvard University Press, 1958), I, p. 193.

8. Stephen Orgel, "Prospero's Wife," *Representations,* 8 (1984), 1–13, is evidence that methodologically sophisticated critics, writing in methodologically sophisticated journals, may be turning back toward the biographical Shakespeare in order to extract greater riches from works such as *The Tempest.* For a fruitful example of speculative biography along more traditional lines, see John Berryman, "Shakespeare at Thirty," in his *The Freedom of the Poet* (New York: Farrar, Straus and Giroux, 1976), pp. 29–55.

9. Foucault, "What is an Author," *passim;* Roland Barthes, "The Death of the Author," in *Image, Music, Text,* trans. Stephen Heath (New York: Hill and Wang, 1977), pp. 142–148. For an earlier view of Shakespeare as a culturally

editor and critic survive long without him? Perhaps (to adapt a theory of Harold Bloom's) neither writing nor reading are adequate experiences unless they are mythologized into a primal scene of instruction, parent to child (and critics, haunted by a sense of their own marginality and belatedness, are only too eager to seize that parental identity for themselves).[10] Common authorial practices suggest an awareness that readers care less about a story if they cannot envision themselves as receiving it from a teller. What is the value of a parable without some suggestion of a wisdom that composed it? Perhaps, for pedagogical purposes, we need to replace the dismissive New Critical category of "the intentional fallacy" with a renewed Romantic category called something like "the intentional mythology," a generative idea of the author built from the demonstrable coherences of the surviving evidence.

Voltaire's maxim comes to mind: if this authorial deity did not exist, it would be necessary to invent him. We turn Shakespeare (back) into a person so that we can keep him as a wise parental god. Shakespeare's historical existence provides a human center for our studies, even while his status as a cultural deity invests our critical and editorial projects with a sort of absolute importance. When we let ourselves think about the plays in terms of their author, we are sliding from criticism, not merely toward history, but also toward religion. (The modern world seems to crave such superhuman authorities because we doubt them, and doubt them because we know how desperately we crave to believe in them.) The relationship between the death of God and the death of the author (asserted by Nietzsche and

determined machine, see Mark Twain, "What is Man?" in his *What is Man? and Other Essays* (New York: Harper and Brothers, 1917), pp. 8–9. This same passage, however, admires Shakespeare's unique talent for processing the material his personal experience provided to him; Twain's point is not that the ideology really writes the plays, but rather that all human thoughts and actions can be understood within a philosophical framework that eliminates credit and blame by eliminating entirely the idea of free will. Even Shelley—though in far more mystical terms—portrays the poet as partly a transmitter of a force beyond himself or herself.

10. Harold Bloom, *A Map of Misreading* (New York: Oxford University Press, 1975), pp. 41–63, discusses writing and instruction in terms of this primal scene.

several of his followers) runs deep in the case of Bardolatry. We often show the symptoms of incomplete mourning in both our critical and our pedagogical practices, persisting in secretly denying these deaths that we have been forced outwardly to acknowledge. Much of what we write on our blackboards and in our scholarly journals amounts to a graffito of protest: "Shakespeare lives!"

Consider the tremendous interest generated recently by the attribution to Shakespeare of a lyric called "Shall I Die?" This was ostensibly a discovery about texts, but it became front-page news only because it was implicitly a statement about Shakespeare himself: he speaks to us from beyond the grave! Behind the attributing editor's assertions of humble and diligent service to Shakespeare lies a gleeful claim to power, based on possession of some extremely private words from the oracle. To this dutiful servant of the Word in the sanctum sanctorum of the Bodleian, a visitation was granted, a prophecy to be carried to the others of the order. The analogy to the missing piece of a treasure-map suggests itself, but what Pearl is the treasure? The editor describes the poem as "awakening from the ancient sheets in which it had lain undisturbed for centuries."[11] Aside from being untrue—the poem has been read and catalogued several times in the interim—this statement is symptomatic in its suggestions of Resurrection, which make the Rawlinson manuscript reminiscent as much of the Shroud of Turin as of the Dead Sea Scrolls. The fervor with which this minor attribution has been asserted and disputed recalls nothing so much as the debates over the authenticity of certain parts of the Bible.[12] This strikes me as more than a casual analogy; the zeal of the combatants,

11. Gary Taylor, "Shakespeare's New Poem: A Scholar's Clues and Conclusions," *New York Times Book Review,* December 15, 1985, pp. 11–14. The presentation of the poem itself in the *Times* was revealing: all in a box, in an italic type-face, as if it were indeed some sort of precious artifact in a reliquary, an artifact by which one might gain new access to a special and mysterious power inherent in the Shakespeareness of being Shakespeare.

12. Foucault, "What Is an Author," p. 127, comments that "Modern criticism, in its desire to 'recover' the author from a work, employs devices strongly reminiscent of Christian exegesis when it wished to prove the value of a text by ascertaining the holiness of its author."

the warnings of blasphemy, and the rituals of canonization all suggest an essentially religious rather than strictly literary controversy.[13]

What motivates this zealous pursuit of Shakespeare's literary and biographical relics is partly the usual editorial quest for accuracy, and partly also the usual human appetite for gossip: why else would scholars who would not dream of picking up *People* magazine, even if trapped in the longest checkout line in supermarket history, regularly exhaust themselves and their fellow scholars with their efforts to establish the true identity of Shakespeare's Dark Lady—that is, the sonnets' Dark Lady? But it is something more, too: whether consciously or not, many Shakespeareans assume that, by acquiring personal information and bringing it to bear on the literature, we can come closer to knowing Shakespeare's knowledge as he knew it himself. We want to be backstage, present before Shakespeare places the veils of literary illusion over the motivating Verity to keep it from blinding ordinary eyes. The modern Shakespeare industry

---

13. The form of the debate about "Shall I Die?" is instructive in another way: it shows that our feelings about Shakespeare—worshipful and protective feelings—cannot be reconciled with our theoretical neutrality toward texts. The first thing most Shakespeareans seem to say about the poem, in private conversation, is that it isn't good enough to be by Shakespeare; publicly, though, the orthodox position is that such a judgment is irrelevant because it is Bardolatrous and historically changeable. Many critics escape this revealing schism between their private and public opinions by asserting (reasonably enough) that they don't finally care whether the poem is by Shakespeare or not, since its weaknesses would make it a negligible addition to the canon. The emphatic blandness of these assertions seems to me to cover an instinctive desire to protect our literary deity from the blemish of having written such inferior verse.

For an editor, of course, the question of attribution is important, and the question of quality practically irrelevant, because he is editing a volume that purports to contain Shakespeare's complete works. (It is worth noting here, however, that the concept of "works" may itself be an arbitrary ideological fiction. As Foucault asks, pp. 118–119, would one include laundry lists, if they were available?) The editing of canonical texts is almost inevitably a flight from belatedness, in the form of a fiction of passive solidarity with the author's original intentions. But what justification do those of us not editing such a volume have for our concern? If we are not interested in Shakespeare as a personality constructed (that is, reconstructed) out of a series of clues known as his works, or as some sort of transcendent cultural hero, what does the attribution matter?

has in fact been built on the implicit promise of a decoding: when we can identify the real themes, and the real text, then maybe we will be able to hear Shakespeare himself speak. Criticism and editing become something akin to religious rituals of purification preparatory to a divine manifestation. Despite the arguments of many semioticians, the codes themselves are not the primary appeal, though they may be the only verifiable object. The "Shakespeare" we study and teach is a Rosetta stone, with both literary works and biographical facts written on it, but our main reason for wanting to be able to translate between the literature and the biography is the hope that a wise and kindly figure has left some covert but ultimately legible message for us in that stone.[14]

This may all prove simply that Shakespeare was a brilliant illusionist, remarkably good at establishing a vanishing point near the seeming center of insight. His plays establish constellations of symmetry and spiderwebs of visual and verbal and thematic connection, all generated with such seeming ease and conviction that he appears to be merely reporting to us on some ultimate artistic Creation, translating into human terms a divine text that we could never have deciphered in its original charactery. Having hinted that Shakespeare possesses this kind of vision, the plays then seem to nominate themselves as metaphoric guides to that vision, like the little parables by which conventional morality is sometimes taught to children. Anyone who perceives Shakespeare as that sort of creator, and that sort of benevolent father, is naturally susceptible to the most extreme forms of Bardolatry.

We as teachers—particularly those of us trained in close reading—therefore face a difficult choice, because we cannot verify the accuracy or even the presence of this underlying wisdom. Even in teaching the dazzling surface patterns of the text as if they were sufficient in themselves, we are likely to encourage students to perceive them as outlines of a magnificent passage

14. Indeed, the stubborn popular belief that authors must be unusually wise and kindly people is itself a symptom of this hope. The sentimental portrait of the author helps to mitigate and disguise the implacable, inhuman authority of the printed word.

through which the author has already traveled, the wake of a voyage toward some ultimate vision, as if art were merely the by-product of some greater undertaking. We must either play along, gazing excitedly into that distance like a prankster who gathers a staring crowd by staring himself at an unremarkable point in the sky; or else we must debunk, pointing to the vanishing point of the emperor's new clothes. (Materialist critics often practice a complex version of the debunking alternative, by emphasizing that these lovely literary fripperies serve mainly to distract us from the role canonical writings usually play in the enforcement of the political status quo.)

Most of us, of course, assure ourselves that between these extremes of enchantment and debunking there lies a middle ground of humble, honest, and productive practice. We work on various bits of the plays with the avowed intention of finally reassembling the cleaned and refurbished parts into a more clearly expressive whole, as if we were reconditioning a typewriter. We devote ourselves to filtering out interference, as if we were attuned to a distant radio signal.[15] But whose writing, whose signal? We seek to demystify the ritual of artistic communication, on the questionable assumption that the ritual is not the essence of the power to which we desire closer access (like a child looking for the "tick" among the scattered pieces of a disembowelled watch). Behind our unassuming editorial and pedagogical practices there still lurks a very big assumption: that if we do this for each of the plays, they can finally be reassembled into a comprehensible and personable Shakespeare.

This pleasant spirit of critical/editorial positivism points simultaneously in two contradictory directions. On the one hand, it suggests that the text is merely a medium, a transparency

---

15. Indeed, to biographical critics, the dramatic elements of drama are sometimes little more than disposable static; to psychoanalytic critics, distortions in the signal, aberrations from simple narrative communication, are themselves the most alluring music, the only text in which the author's true self becomes legible. It should be noted here that an increasingly prominent editorial trend emphasizes the instability of the text, the impossibility of perfecting it. The text becomes, not a transparency, but a sort of kaleidoscope through which we see the author, if at all, darkly and multiply.

through which Shakespeare himself may finally become fully visible. On the other hand, it suggests that the text is a self-sufficient entity, opaque and perfectible, and that the ideal edition of the plays would be something like those annotated Bibles that, rather than presuming to analyze sources or meanings, offer merely maps, genealogies, and an index to the places in the text where immutable and infallible moral advice on a variety of questions can supposedly be found. (The recent emphasis on treating the plays as practical theater, both in criticism and in the classroom, makes sense partly as a way around several of these problems.) Is there a way to teach Shakespeare's works without thus pretending either that we can know the author as a human being, or else that he never existed as one? Is it worth attempting to harness students' natural fascination with Shakespeare as both a historical person and a cultural oracle? What is lost if we obey contemporary theory and exclude our thinking about Shakespeare's historical self from our thinking and teaching about Shakespeare's writings?

Two recent experiences provoked me to ponder this last question. A man sitting next to me on an airplane paused from his drink to ask me what I was doing, and I told him, not very patiently, that I was revising a draft of an article on Shakespeare. The idea of literary criticism was clearly an unfamiliar one to him—he was a construction worker, he said—and he fell silent for a few minutes, staring out the window; but then he asked, in an uncertain voice, "What did Shakespeare think about marriage—you know, between a man and a woman?" Precisely what sort of an emotional scene this man was returning from, or on his way to, I couldn't know, but clearly he wanted advice from a sanctioned voice of timeless wisdom about human dealings, from a god who spoke in parables. In my identity as a critic, I was being called upon to serve as hierophant. "Speak to it, Horatio," he might as well have said, "thou art a scholar."

From the podium at a conference of critics, I would of course have answered that Shakespeare's plays are all different, that none of them can be defined as Shakespeare himself speaking, nor can what is spoken be taken as an instruction about conduct; if any message is there, no one can state with perfect objectivity what it is. But on the overnight flight into Boston, I told him a few things many Shakespeareans, if pressed, would say in some form—about the struggle to transform the emotional bonds of childhood into heterosexual love, about the power of love to preserve marriage through trust, and of marriage (though it is perpetually on the brink of tragedy) to offer a form of immortality through procreation. He nodded thoughtfully and let me go back to my task, but it did not seem to be quite the same task I had left a few minutes earlier.

A few months later, after a Royal Shakespeare Company performance of *Hamlet* one cold and foggy night in Stratford, England, I walked back up along the Avon to Trinity Church, and stood among the stones in the churchyard, in a surprisingly successful effort to spook myself. It was one of those intensely private moments we seek out so that we can tell people about them, and this is my opportunity. I was trying to contact the shade of Shakespeare, trying, by pressing my forehead against the wall of the church nearest his grave, to conjure some sort of explanatory ghost. After a few minutes of frustration, I turned away—and saw the Stratford playhouse glowing in the distance through the fog. I had spent the whole evening in the company of a very lively and informative ghost who had spoken to me in the most expressive terms it could find. Anything I could add to that message at Trinity Church would be both literally and figuratively a relic, a scrap of the skeleton Shakespeare's epitaph so chillingly urges us not to remove. I was not convinced, exactly, that the author is the text, but it did seem obvious that the part of the author that matters to us is derived from, and largely coextensive with, the text.[16]

16. Compare the experience John Updike describes in his essay "On Meeting Writers," in his *Picked-up Pieces* (Greenwich, Ct.: Fawcett Books, 1966), p. 21. Updike tells of attending a lecture by T. S. Eliot, pressing forward at the end to make contact with the great genius, and encountering merely a weary man—a shell from which readers already had the precious essence. From a Bardolatrous perspective, my experience is reminiscent of those Christian Reformation narratives—Herbert's "Redemption" or Vaughan's "The Search," for example—that portray a long misguided pursuit of God's physical presence. This pursuit finally yields to the recognition of a new sort of God who offers a new sort of presence: not among, but within us, not in pieces of wood or patches of desert, but in the hearts and minds of humankind.

The first incident confirmed that the idea of an author who communicates through his works is still useful; the second added a warning, that the search for that author may nonetheless become misguided when it is pursued with literal-minded fervor. The idea of Shakespeare makes something valuable about the plays available in ways that a strict textuality forbids. The danger is that this idea (since it quickly accretes alluring fictional elements) can easily seize precedence over the plays in an undisciplined imagination. The study of Shakespeare the man risks implying that, while the plays may be impressive or enjoyable in their own rights, they essentially serve as advertisements for a guru.

Fear of encouraging that inference has driven me to the point of telling students that there are only two things one really needs to know about Shakespeare the man in order to appreciate Shakespeare the author, and that both are things one learns from the plays rather than from the biography. The first is that he was a human being much like the rest of us, a person who knew just what it was like (for example) to hate going to school in the morning. The second is that he was totally unlike any of the rest of us, an utterly transparent medium through which every human trait and experience could speak with perfect clarity.[17]

Because Shakespeare was a person like us, he spoke to feelings like ours—or, to be more precise, I conclude he was a person like us because he seems to me to speak to those feelings so frequently and powerfully. Ben Jonson's famous eulogy describing Shakespeare as "not of an age, but for all time" sounds rather hollow in a classroom today, an echo from a bygone time of complacent humanistic Bardolatry, a cliché that runs against contemporary insights that have come to historicize Shakespeare, not to praise him. But isn't it possible that Jonson—himself a great believer in realism and the contemporary—was right in crediting Shakespeare with transcending those things?

17. Jorge Luis Borges, "Everything and Nothing," in *Labyrinths* (New York: New Directions, 1964), pp. 248–249, is impelled by this quality of transparency to make explicit the deification of Shakespeare that is implicit in the works of more cautious interpreters.

Allowing for certain ethnocentrisms and factors of gender, Shakespearean drama speaks, in heightened and sharpened terms, to some primary human feelings that are historically stable and virtually universal, given the stability and universality of certain instincts and appetites, and the basic ineluctable facts of birth and death. It is also possible to credit Shakespeare with the same kind of insight into the basic tensions of social organization on a larger scale, but he was certainly not a mere spokesman (however eloquent) for the class system in the abstract, or for the ideas and instincts that oppose it; nor did he merely condense the dialogue between those mighty opposites in his society. His works are not primarily manifestations of the symbolic, even theatrical, forms of authority on which Elizabethan society depended, nor are they primarily examples of language and literature expressing doubts about their own capacity for coherent meaning. They are, I believe, the efforts of a person to tell good stories to good effect, to mirror life in ways that compel audiences to consider what they share with the apparently human characters and, on a deeper level of analysis, with the posited human author.

This sort of grand Romantic assertion about the value of Shakespeare is risky. It can be dismissed as the merest personal preference, or historicized until the teacher seems no more authentically autonomous than the author. Shakespeareans with different orientations—materialist, post-structuralist, Lacanian—may develop viable classroom strategies consonant with their critical theories. But teaching a class necessarily entails accepting one theoretical premise or another, even if only tentatively and implicitly; and, for now, these are the conclusions about Shakespeare-as-author that shape my pedagogical choices.

My view of Shakespearean drama encourages me to use analogies to modern life and culture in an effort to make the works seem relevant to the students' own lives. This sort of approach has fallen into disfavor in the reaction against the teaching experiments of the late 1960s, but there was a baby in that discarded bathwater. Shakespeare's plays have endured so well largely because they do this sort of teaching themselves; the grand melodramatic crises faced by the great Shakespearean heroes tend to be recognizable analogues to the real ordinary problems faced by real ordinary people in their inner lives, however different their outer lives may seem. If Shakespeare was perfectly willing to talk to the Elizabethans about personal and political choices through the stories of Coriolanus and Julius Caesar, we should be willing to talk about Shakespeare's Coriolanus and Julius Caesar through stories of our own personal and political worlds. Though we are not medieval Danish princes told by ghosts to kill our uncles, many of us have felt bewildered and betrayed to discover sexuality, hypocrisy, and mortality in our formerly idolized parents. We may not be medieval Scottish thanes incited by witches to usurp kings, but we are still haunted by rash selfish desires that tempt us to less vivid but no less fated and sinister violations of supposedly benevolent orders in society and nature.

Psychoanalytic criticism has a place in the classroom for a similar reason: not because Shakespeare was secretly writing prescient psychoanalysis, or because Hamlet and Macbeth are real people pursuing Oedipal desires for which their visible fears and deeds are merely symptoms or substitutes, but rather because Shakespeare induces in his readers and spectators a compelling subliminal identification with the desires and anger and guilt of these characters by encoding within the tragic situations a version of normal psychological tensions. Neither the grand dramatic situation nor its ordinary psychological counterpart is merely a symbol or a cover for the other; much of Shakespeare's power lies in his genius for creating situations in which these two levels remain perfectly aligned. At the risk again of aggrandizing the Shakespeare professor into a surrogate Shakespeare, I conclude that good teaching of Shakespeare should use the same correspondences, should tap the same sources within the audience that Shakespeare himself so successfully tapped. By offering analogies between the situations depicted in the plays and emotional or psychological situations commonly faced by the students, a teacher can legitimately accomplish that, in a way resembling the way Shakespeare arguably reached *his* audiences.

Showing students that the personalities and experiences depicted in the plays are not so foreign as they might at first seem is a necessary antidote to the cold and fearful response evoked by antique language and antique settings, particularly in art-works that carry such immense cultural prestige. Teachers of literature are almost inevitably translators; when the literature is centuries old, another layer of translation is added. Unless we work rather freely from the apparent source, the writings are likely to lose their impact, even their coherence, through this chain of transmission. So if *King Lear* is a good way to talk about the inevitable and unbearable facts of mortality and loss, and those mortal losses a good way to talk about *King Lear,* why should we shun that dialogue? "Popularizing" comparisons, say, between Coriolanus and scholarship athletes, or even between Angelo and television evangelists, are not necessarily pernicious. Movies and television programs offer fruitful points of comparison to some situations and effects in Elizabethan drama—which apparently held a similar place in popular culture. Shakespeare's works and their modern analogues are not the same thing, of course, but education does not proceed by perfect identities.

In seeking to isolate evocative modern analogues to the chief emotional energies of the plays, I also invite the accusation of "thematizing," a pejorative term suggesting that any discussion of "main themes" provides an *illusion* of coherence, and reduces the complexities of literary expression to mere argument by selecting and foregrounding certain aspects of the work apart from the whole. But if that theoretical objection is rigorously obeyed, the alternative seems to be a deconstructionist strategy that does the same sort of thing in a more costly way, isolating and emphasizing tensions and discontinuities within the text so as to exclude any coherent Shakespearean consciousness from the writing that appears under his name. A criticism that considers itself too intelligent, advanced, and self-aware to acknowledge the moral implications and emotional evocations that have provoked such wide and deep interest in Shakespearean drama through centuries of changing attitudes toward literature and interpretation, may help to raise consciousness about some paradoxes in the study of linguistics, but it is hard to see how it accomplishes the task of teaching Shakespeare.

My strategy for conjuring a personable and powerful Shakespeare into the classroom is vulnerable to attack from several other theoretical perspectives as well. My emphasis on enriching ordinary experience risks merely replacing the "Shakespeare, Lad of Stratford" lecture with the no less hackneyed "Humanities, Builder of Souls" lecture. This genre has become compromised by the contradiction between two ideas about how souls should be built. On the one hand, there is the tweedy old notion of preparing the professional class for their moments of leisure when, sitting in wingback chairs in paneled libraries, wearing silk paisley smoking jackets, they can nod in sage assent to leather-bound copies of Shakespeare's works, drawing spiritual sustenance amid a barbarous world. On the other hand, there is a more recent, denim-clad notion that the humanities are an opportunity to nurture radical idealisms, and that students who are taught Shakespeare properly will pass their lives in a state of intense emotional and ethical alertness.[18]

The main attack on the sentimental humanistic approach comes from the latter camp: critics who feel that criticism should be used for political advocacy—or, more precisely, that until now it has been subtly used for the wrong kind of political advocacy. The study of Shakespeare has at times been consciously and unabashedly employed against the forces of cultural diversity, as the dedicatory address at the opening of the Folger Library in 1932 clearly demonstrates.[19] My supposition that we are somehow teaching "humanity" when we teach "Shakespeare" is fraught with disquieting implications, in political as well as strictly critical terms. It involves some assumptions that are widely considered ideologically retrograde, politically incorrect: that human beings, across historical periods and class levels, have essential

18. It is worth keeping in mind, however, the warning of one famous radical literary critic in the late 1960s, who argued in a conversation that undergraduates should not be taught Shakespeare at all, because his elusiveness and relentless ambiguity on ethical questions would necessarily interfere with the development of confident, violent radicalism. The spectacle of Hamlet trying to play a role in some Wittenberg branch of the S.D.S. would certainly be interesting to watch.

19. Stephen J. Brown, "The Uses of Shakespeare in America: A Study in Class Domination," in *Shakespeare: Pattern of Excelling Nature*, ed. David Bevington and Jay L. Halio (Cranbury, N.J.: Associated University Presses, 1978), pp. 230–238, discusses the repressive implications of Joseph Quincy Adams' remarkable speech.

characteristics, needs, and sufferings in common. Marxist critics such as Terry Eagleton have suggested that the old-fashioned claim that great literature teaches eternal and beautiful human verities is part of a bourgeois conspiracy designed, at a particular moment in English history, to make education and literature safe for the class system, by making what were really (or potentially) subversive literary representations of class struggle into isolated aesthetic artifacts (through the close readings of New Criticism), or lessons in the absolute truth of what were in fact the values of only a certain comfortable class of white Western European males (through the sonorous pieties of old-line humanism).[20]

But the approaches to teaching Shakespeare generated by these openly political theories of criticism have important weaknesses, precisely because of the ways they distance Shakespeare from the teaching of his works. Most Marxist critics believe no less than I do in positing a true source for the plays and then establishing relevance to the students' contemporary world, but both the source they posit and the relevance they emphasize have to do with the dynamics of the economic system as a whole rather than the hearts and minds of autonomous individuals. Those who give primacy to the dynamics of class struggle, and who mistrust the idea of private property, necessarily resist the notion that the author produces his or her work independently and retains some special rights over it. Furthermore, the current British school of "cultural materialist" Shakespeare criticism generally makes no pretense of accepting the plays within their own world. For these critics, Renaissance England is important as a body-politic distinct from ours yet suffering from remarkably similar symptoms; Shakespeare's works serve to document the class struggle, the centralization of state power, and the emergence of modern capitalism at a crucial stage where their traits are starkly visible. This line of analysis leads to a particular

---

20. Terry Eagleton, *Literary Theory: An Introduction* (Minneapolis: University of Minnesota Press, 1983). In fact, a Marxist critic might argue that my emphasis on the individual author as the creator of literature, and my sentimental notion of humanistic education in which literature is a tool, help to expose each other as symptoms of a capitalistic ideology.

form of teaching, but what it chiefly teaches is not "Shakespeare," but rather a predetermined political lesson that Shakespeare can be made to exemplify. The chief debates within the movement are about what balance of ambivalence the works suggest toward the ruling ideology—that is, to what extent they are implicated in the repressive system and to what extent they deliberately subvert it—and (more subtly) about the extent to which such literary or ritual subversion is actually containment, to what extent it subserves the hierarchical system it purports to attack. The conclusion may vary from play to play. Though works such as *Merchant of Venice* and *The Tempest* seem usefully aware of the flaws in capitalism and colonialism, others such as *Taming of the Shrew* and *Cymbeline* are considered so badly compromised by subtle alliance with the premises of the social hierarchy as to be too dangerous for anything but the most emotionally distant and dismissive analysis, in which they become expressions of the authoritarian system that demanded them, rather than of any free-willed author who created them.

The movement in Renaissance studies in America known as the New Historicism—ostensibly a major ally of the young British Marxists—is virtually the opposite of the British movement in one important respect: it tends to make the ideology of Elizabethan England a distant intellectual puzzle rather than an immediate call to action. (The relatively grim economic and political situation of Britain in the 1980s, especially for young scholars in the humanities, may help to explain the different degrees of activism). New Historicism treats Shakespeare's works primarily as the artifacts of an alien culture, as symptoms of the peculiar symbolic ideology by which power expressed and asserted itself in the English Renaissance. My concern is that this school of thought distances its students from Shakespeare in its own way. Given its emphasis on transcribing and deciphering the bizarre, intricate codes by which political authority asserted and sustained itself in the Elizabethan world, New Historicist teaching must tend to present the plays as evidence of the great foreignness of Shakespeare's culture, must necessarily focus its attention on anecdotes that suggest how strangely different the transactions portrayed and fostered by the plays must be from any of our own. To see that culture in its most characteristic

activities is to find and emphasize those aspects that are *not* true
in our culture as well. This can provide a striking lesson in
history and ideological shaping, but it threatens to rob Shakespearean drama of its real accessibility and relevance, by creating too elaborate a conceptual mediation between the world
in which the students live, and the one in which they are encouraged to place the plays.

My point, then, is that it should be possible to teach and learn
a great deal from and about Shakespeare's works without either
(as New Historicists generally do) exaggerating our distance
from the forces that generated those works and therefore from
Shakespeare, or (as cultural materialists generally do) eradi-
cating the historical distance on the grounds that reading Shakespeare in his own terms is irrelevant, because the plays are most
useful as raw material for an analysis of contemporary capitalism
and the class system, or even dangerous, because the plays serve
to inscribe those repressive structures. We need a way of teaching Shakespeare that can connect some plausible version of the
original sentiments of the work (located in the author as well
as in the world that shaped that author) with the experiences
of most modern students. That need is not answered by making
the plays conform to a leveling ideology any more than it was
by making them conform to a hierarchical chain-of-being ideology. Either way, the individual consciousness of the author is
effaced, compromising the responsiveness of the works to the
emotions of the individual spectator, reader, or student.

Certainly my approach can be attacked as ahistorical—that
is, as pretending to be ahistorical. But the answer is not to
surrender the literary experience wholly to history, to treat the
work as primarily an artifact of the political system (or, indeed,
the linguistic system) amid which it arose. The postulated author, the sentimental idea of a Shakespeare, allows us to focus
on the particular emotional experience represented, and evoked
in us, by the drama. To accept the increasingly popular notion
that the cultural ideology rather than the individual author creates the literary work is to doom any such response before it
begins, to forbid the impression that the play constitutes a communication from one person to others about something they
share as sentient individuals. My appreciation of Shakespeare,

admittedly, constitutes a communication between two literate upper-middle-class white males in postfeudal Western European cultures. The corridor I have tested is thus far too narrow to justify my saying that Shakespeare's works speak to universals of human experience. But by contriving to communicate, with what I can muster of passion and humor, what Shakespeare makes me feel about my own life, I seem to be able to increase the interest of most students (including those of another social class, race, or gender) in reading Shakespeare, and perhaps even their capacities for feeling and expressing passion and humor. Even if I cannot prove that I am precisely "teaching Shakespeare"—or deny that institutional coercion plays a role in these student responses—that certainly seems worthwhile.

Amid all this rather abstract and prescriptive argument, it should be noted that good teachers—of Shakespeare or nearly anything else—are so because they have a talent for teaching itself, not because their approach to literature is sound from all the latest theoretical perspectives. It is a poor craftsman, the proverb tells us, who blames his tools. Furthermore, plays such as *King Lear* create the rare situation in which the teaching of morals and emotions becomes virtually inextricable from the teaching of an academic subject. The question is whether this represents a wonderful opportunity, even an obligation, or whether instead it constitutes a diabolical temptation to abandon our critical precepts and abuse our professorial authority by propounding our own views and attributing them to Shakespeare's authoritative voice.

One thing good teachers can convey vividly without obviously forfeiting political neutrality is that they themselves find pleasure, excitement, interest, humor, and consolation in their fields of learning. When students admire someone who seems genuinely to love the topic, they attempt to discover for themselves such an obviously rewarding love. But conveying a love of Shakespeare in any extensive and articulate way, rather than merely by example, requires the development of a sort of *lingua franca* between the Elizabethan world and ours. That means not only talking about theatrical conventions and glossing difficult words and phrases, but showing how the emotional situations that appear in such extreme and archaic forms within the plays translate into ordinary modern lives, showing that the plays speak from and to the shared pain for our mortal being.

Some of my argument may be misconstrued as anti-intellectual, as a betrayal of the challenges of modern thought, and a condescension to the abilities of the modern college student. I certainly do not mean to argue that we should concentrate on making Shakespeare easy; I mean we should do what we can to make Shakespeare vivid, so students can have the full benefit of his difficulty. We need to clear away certain obstacles and confusions created by the passing of time that have no relation to the original spirit of the work, so students can confront the obstacles and confusions that do. While there is no valid reason for applying to Shakespeare only those terminologies he might conceivably have applied to himself, I believe that theoretical approaches to Shakespeare engage students most effectively and authentically when the theories still have some of the momentum and flexibility of the drama itself behind it, and correspond to a mode of thought that was plausibly active in the author. So I teach *Hamlet* partly in terms of hermeneutic and epistemological problems; *Much Ado, Romeo and Juliet, Othello,* and *Antony and Cleopatra* also specifically invite us to ponder further the nature of misreading and the indeterminacy of meaning. My teaching of *Macbeth* and *Coriolanus,* even in the most basic sort of survey course, leans heavily on Freudian and post-Freudian psychoanalysis, because the protagonists' relations with the central women in their life respond very richly to those approaches, and the extremities of infantile experience offer a bridge between the violence and violations on stage and the common psychic experiences of students and audiences.

My approach includes historical as well as theoretical elements. This involves more than either repeating or repudiating a third traditional opening Shakespeare lecture, the "Renaissance, Age of Splendor" lecture, which usually implies that imperial exploration and scientific inventions in the period necessarily correlated with great artistic discoveries, and usually treats a portrait of Queen Elizabeth in jewelry and a woodcut of the Spanish Armada in trouble as sufficient illustration of England's "golden age," ignoring the terrible struggles of most Elizabethans against the extensive miseries of disease and poverty.[21] My teaching of *Macbeth*, for example, has heavy New Historicist overtones, because the evident ambivalence toward Macbeth's fatedness suggests analogies to the double bind imposed on Shakespeare and his contemporaries by the mixed messages of a culture that at once exalted and condemned ambition, that portrayed humanity simultaneously as a great conqueror and a hopelessly depraved victim, that expelled people from their former roles in a social economy yet punished them for seeking new ones. The play thus corresponds suggestively to a world that in its official proclamations condemned any political unrest as a crime against nature, even while constantly acknowledging in subtler ways that human beings were inevitably at war with the orders of nature.

Nor is my approach necessarily apolitical. Current social controversies often come under discussion, usually because they were evidently current for Shakespeare as well. Capitalism is an active issue in *Merchant of Venice*, imperialism in *The Tempest*, fascism in *Coriolanus;* analyzing these plays demands analyzing these topics, not because all criticism has a political valence, but because the topics are prominent features of the plays, because the tensions testing the central characters bear noteworthy resemblances to important tensions in the political economy of Renaissance England. I tell students that *Othello* is not exactly a play about racism, but that it does explore the way racist stereotypes can destroy our loving faith in ourselves and in others, that racism becomes one of the various latent social evils Iago so skillfully elicits and enlists, and that the play's imagery of light and dark therefore does not exist in some sort of aesthetic vacuum.

Teaching virtually any of Shakespeare's plays requires teaching, to some extent, feminist theory, as a way of understanding the comic dilemmas of a Viola or the tragic ones of a Cleopatra.

21. Political critics of Shakespeare often practice, even more extensively than I do, this sort of historical revisionism. For all its professed populist tendencies, however, most New Historicist teaching and criticism—unlike the work of practical historians in recent years—has maintained a comfortable distance from the concrete facts of life in the underclass, preferring to perform its own symbolic readings of those royal portraits, seemingly still mesmerized by the symbols of privilege and power it purports to debunk.

The plays offer active critiques of the destructive ways men perceive women: as inherently frail and vain (morally as well as physically), as primal betrayers who sow discord between men-friends, and as sinister enchanters (when often the men are merely projecting their own disturbing desires). At other times, however, it seems important to go beyond, or at least outside, what is demonstrably in the play, to place Shakespeare within an ideology we disbelieve or dislike.[22] Though *Hamlet* and *The Winter's Tale* may strike us as enlightened diagnoses of the injustices imposed on wives in a patriarchal culture, *Taming of the Shrew* may strike us as merely a symptom of that disease that threatens contagion. As statements explicitly *built onto* a reading of the play itself, such objections can be valid, valuable, even obligatory. But condemning the ethos of a play, no less than exalting it, requires positing a creating consciousness; it involves defining the discrepancies between an attitude the play represents and an attitude we hope our students will adopt. I certainly stress to my students their dual obligation, to participate as fully as they can in the mentality of the world in which the artwork was created and afterwards to criticize the aspects of the work that cultural change has taught us are scientifically incorrect, ethically repugnant, or socially unhealthy. With explicitly political problems in the study of Shakespearean drama, as with the more subtly political problem of the nature of the author-function, the question is how to be responsible teachers without being irresponsible critics. This two-stage approach is the closest I have come to an answer.

In another, broader sense, my approach is anything but apolitical. If "Poets are the unacknowledged legislators of the world," as Shelley asserts, then by helping students empathize with characters and situations that at first appeared foreign to them, we canvass for the best sort of poetic legislation: "The great secret of morals is love; or a going out of our own nature, and an identification of ourselves with the beautiful which exists in

22. Peter Erickson, "Shakespeare and the 'Author-Function,' " in *Shakespeare's Rough Magic,* ed. Peter Erickson and Coppélia Kahn (Newark: University of Delaware Press, 1985), offers an excellent discussion of the problems of "placing" the author, particularly in regard to feminist issues.

thought, action, or person, not our own. A man, to be greatly good, must imagine intensely and comprehensively; he must put himself in the place of another and of many others; the pains and pleasures of his species must become his own."[23] A teacher who enables students to identify with the pains and pleasures of Shakespeare's characters augments the political morality of a state in much the same way I believe the plays themselves do—by fostering the consciousness that must underlie good political choices, rather than advocating particular policies that changing circumstances may render unjust, or reveal to be misguided.

A humanistic approach may thus have a reformist or even revolutionary influence, even while it appears to be serving a bourgeois agenda. It is one thing to say that all criticism—indeed, all teaching—exists within a political matrix, and has political consequences. It is quite another to conclude by a faulty syllogism that all criticism and teaching therefore is, should be, nothing *but* politics. Choosing a sexual partner (or a god, or a meal) almost always has political implications, but that does not mean that the entirety of the motives and the experience can be understood and conveyed through a purely political analysis. Aesthetic and emotionalistic observations about the plays may conceivably deflect attention from social injustices and contribute to a quietistic attitude that generally helps preserve the political status quo; that does not mean that such observations are completely unreal or unhealthy, or even that they are made with the *purpose* of preserving the status quo—the authorial hand as velvet fist.

The alternative for activist critics is merely to use, as a jumping-off place for political advocacy, the spots in the plays that provide the best footing. Some who would scoff at the simplism of teaching *Romeo and Juliet* as a pretty tribute to the splendor of true love or *Macbeth* as an admirable warning about the wickedness of ambition (especially in women) seem surprisingly willing to portray those same plays as devastating condemnations of the depredations and depravities of decadent aristocratic and monarchical systems (especially as operated by men). The

23. Shelley, "Defence," II, p. 11.

fact that this approach reduces the experience of these plays to a single argument is not necessarily altered by the fact that it is now a more modern and politically enlightened single argument.

It is presumptuous to assume that we know what specific political causes the plays should be made to serve—to assume that, in this regard, we know better than Shakespeare. Such advocacy does not simply update *what* Shakespeare taught; it changes *how* Shakespeare taught. Shakespeare's plays appear to me to be devices ideally suited to instruct and delight their audiences by taking them on vivid expeditions through heightened versions of individual human emotional experience; they are perfect media in which to nurture something like Shelley's "sympathetic imagination." The absence of any explicit leftist agenda in the plays can perhaps be attributed to censorship, but that is at best a partial answer, and one that translates the plays through a posited author even more emphatically than the old-fashioned appeal to humanistic values. Instead, one may conclude that Shakespeare, so to speak, took care of the pennies and let the pounds take care of themselves—assumed that he could accomplish more by sensitizing individual souls than by advocating a particular political position on either the right or the left. Is Tate's complacent *King Lear* better than Shakespeare's because its system of rewards encourages human kindness and obedience more directly? Or, on the other wing, is Brecht's Marxist adaptation of *Coriolanus* finally a more humane document than Shakespeare's original? If we believe that Shakespeare chose to educate further back on the chain of deduction, before the enacted experiences translated into a set of senatorial or parliamentary resolutions, then we are under some obligation to take the same approach. Otherwise we are evidently judging ourselves more pedagogically wise and morally alert than one of the most versatile and resilient teachers in the history of Western culture, simply because we are more thoroughly modern.

What we should teach as "Shakespeare" finally depends more on what we mean by teaching than on what we mean by Shakespeare. If the object of a Shakespeare course is to exemplify a theoretically defensible system of critical and editorial practice, then we had best leave the author in his grave. But if we believe that our job entails using literature to encourage a recognition of both the sacred variety and the sacred unity of human experience, then we may be justified in conjuring a ghost of Shakespeare for our students, a spirit that (like old Hamlet) sets our task by crying out, "Remember me!" Whether we consider that phantasm essentially a fiction or a reasonable extrapolation (a sort of docu-drama), it offers a helpful locus of thought that corresponds to, even though it cannot recreate, the historical creature who evidently generated the plays. Shakespeare is dead; long live "Shakespeare"!

We must not, of course, delude ourselves into thinking that there is only one Shakespeare, merely because there only *was* one. No two of us have exactly the same Shakespeare, any more than we have exactly the same *Othello*. Furthermore, we each have several Shakespeares: Shakespeare the cultural celebrity, Shakespeare the extrapolated author, Shakespeare the historical man, and Shakespeare the oracular god. Keeping these figures distinct in our minds seems to me an important step toward understanding what we mean when we say that we "teach Shakespeare."

So "what is needed now" in the teaching of Shakespeare (aside from instinctively good teachers and universities that support them) is an alertness to the methodological implications of what we are doing, an awareness of where our classroom practice has fallen out of step with our scholarly critical theories—but always tempered with a healthy skepticism about the idea that theory is necessarily closer to truth and virtue than practice is. Exclusively foregrounding historical changes, or political theories, or linguistic uncertainties, or aesthetic refinements—as important as each of those things may be—puts most students at an emotional distance from the primary experience of drama. In teaching literary analysis, we risk teaching too much detachment. We still need to make students feel that Shakespearean drama can be real and relevant to them, that Shakespeare will teach them not only about the Renaissance, not only about the class struggle in the abstract, not only about Shakespeare himself, even, but about the experience of their own lives that they share with the large portion of humanity to and for whom Shakespeare speaks so powerfully. We must not let the abstruseness and theoretical exclusiveness to which the exigencies of professional competition have pressed us prevent us from making available to students the Shakespeare that drew us in, that has drawn in audiences and readers for centuries. Nor should we be so perversely, false-humbly egalitarian that we insist on talking to our undergraduate students the same way we address our most learned fellow-Shakespeareans, even though we may be talking about the same basic issues in both conversations.

We need, not a way of teaching that obeys the latest exclusions invented by theory, but rather a theory of teaching that does not forbid us to teach Shakespeare, the Shakespeare we feel we know, the Shakespeare we feel others ought to know, whether for their ethical reform, their aesthetic pleasure, or their intellectual development—whatever it is we believe, as teachers and fellow human beings, is important. We need to sustain the embattled belief that critics can and should aim primarily at assisting authors in their complex efforts to communicate; and to do so, we need to believe in authors as well as author-functions. According to Keats, the writing of Shakespearean drama required an ability to be "in uncertainties, Mysteries, doubts, without any irritable reaching after fact & reason";[24] perhaps we need a "negative capability" in our teaching that will permit us to live with uncertain intentions, a mysterious author, and doubtful meanings, without any irritable reaching after theoretical purity. The "Shakespeare" many people still teach may be essentially a value-laden, humanistic myth. But myths are not lies; they are among the most enduring, most pleasurable, most profound ways of teaching.

24. Keats, *The Letters,* I, p. 193.

JUDITH N. SHKLAR

Why Teach Political Theory?

This essay is not about teaching any specific subject. It is about teaching itself. If some imaginary dean were to ask me why I should be paid to teach political theory, I would naturally offer him only the most conventional reasons for pursuing my vocation. First of all I would remind him that one of the main purposes of a liberal education is to integrate the young into the literary culture of our society. And no one would argue that the history of political theory is marginal to our intellectual heritage, to our collective self-understanding, or to a sense of the continuing presence of the past. Just about every university course that contributes to the general education of our students, whether it deals with literature, the fine arts or the human sciences, invariably has a political theory component—often, it must be said, rather crudely handled. The subject simply insinuates itself into every intellectual corner. Clearly there is a real need to have it taught properly, since it must be a part of an educated person's repertory. Among the ways of learning how to think coherently and critically about politics, none is better than the study of the great authors from Thucydides to the present. Self-education will, in this case, fail. The autodidact always misses the obvious and the insulated analyst of concepts is always in danger of reinventing a primitive version of the wheel. He may also become the prisoner of a single vocabulary, which would be a disaster, given that our accumulated political notions constitute a veritable Tower of Babel. The only way to avoid banality is to encounter, in an intense way, the intellectually wholly other, and to discover how superior to the present and the familiar the utterly remote can be. What could be more challenging than Plato? On the practical side, I would then point out to the now subdued dean, that reading books is not enough, and that there must be a personal exchange for deep learning to actually take place. A teacher must be visibly there to move the students in the first place and then prove to them that a sane and intelligent adult can really care deeply about such things as the history of political thought. It is an Emersonian act of representation, in which the teacher gets the young to recognize and become part of a wide intellectual world, but also accepts that the questions and demands of individual students require respectful answers, and even occasionally a rethinking of received wisdom, especially one's own. Such, then, would be the perfectly sound and not unconvincing talk I would give in my official capacity. I would walk away perhaps richer, but also quite ashamed of myself. For while I would not have lied, I would not have been entirely truthful either. I would not have told the dean what it may not be his business to know, why I *really* teach political theory, or, indeed, why anyone teaches any canon of great literature.

The only reason for teaching political theory is that one is utterly, and possibly irrationally convinced that it is enormously important—and one loves it. It is not for the sake of the students and not even for one's own, apart from one's intellectual obsession, that one can, year after year, think and think about, and explain and explain the contents of books written unimaginably long ago. It is a complex response to a primary passion. Something has set it off, possibly an ideology to which one is committed or its collapse, or historical experience, such as the Second World War lived in Europe or the Depression in America, or the felt need to find new political expressions for an altered and only half understood political world. In any case there must be some personally experienced public events to create an enduring interest in asking the vital question, "how can one think about this at all?" If that becomes an unshakable preoccupation and a passionate quest, then one will teach political theory. In different, but related ways I believe this to be true of all literary studies.

There are easier and betters ways of making a living than teaching, and prestige and fame are not among its rewards. It does not recommend itself as a way of getting on in the world. One may enjoy the company of young people, and good teachers usually do, but the relations between students and teachers are highly stylized and brief. To enter upon an academic career because one thinks that it offers an attractive, genteel, and untroubled "life style" is to head for Waterloo. Unless one is emotionally absorbed in one's subject, teaching is dull, and the normal irritations of academic life may become intolerable. To look forward to a career of being a general all-purpose mentor to the young, or worse, an eternal undergraduate, is to court self-contempt, intellectual decay, and the condescending pity of one's younger colleagues. Even the young become tiresome as the difference in age grows greater. One loses the sense of their individuality and begins to treat them as instances of the same category of being. Such impersonality may bother the student, but it may be less damaging than the too personal manner of teaching in which the bull-session and manipulation replace teaching. In short, unless the impulse to teach is generated by the love of the subject, political theory in this case, it must fail for both the teacher and the student. Nothing else can make the flow of students through the classroom, the seminar, and one's study worthwhile. For the teacher there has to be an enduring intellectual incentive, for the student, something more genuine than mild entertainment. To teach this literature as if it were a precious gift that one gives to every new generation of students, one must really want to read it over and over oneself, because each reading reveals new possibilities, new perceptions, and new ideas. If there is nothing exciting in those books for the teacher, there won't be anything interesting in them for the students either. And if the teacher creates unresponsive students, she cannot expect to get the one thing they can contribute to our mutual encounters: questions and challenges. Nor will the teacher have the occasional pleasure of seeing an immature mind become absolutely accomplished.

The only reason to teach political theory is the conviction that a complete person must be able to think intelligently about government, and that the only way to rise above banality is to learn to think one's way through the works of the great writers on the subject and to learn to argue with them. To see how political ideas fit into the republic of letters generally, into the political systems within which they took place, and finally to see what is dead and alive within this accumulated wealth of psychological and social speculation is to be intellectually transformed, and to have something completely and immediately relevant to think about at any time of the day. If I did not believe that, I would quit teaching at once and go into business.

Someone might suggest that writing offers a better way to tell the world about political theory and especially to contribute something directly to it. This is not the trivial and commonplace notion that, given the limits of time, one should do one's "own work," or "research," rather than teach. Teaching students is as much one's own work as anything can be, and research is something that natural scientists do. Very little if anything that a political theorist does can be described as an addition to factual knowledge about the world, as experimentation or as discovery. It is therefore pretentious and silly for us to talk about a conflict between the demands of research and teaching. If there is a choice to be made at all, it is between two modes of teaching. And while it is true that life is short, I do not see why there should be a particularly great difficulty in dividing one's time between two kinds of teaching and any of the other things one might want to do. Time is not, I suspect, the real issue at all. It is merely a way of talking about the fact that some teachers cannot and do not write anything at all, or nothing worth reading. In fact, there are two ways of teaching, directly and indirectly, and both are psychologically necessary for a full scholarly life because they make different demands upon the teacher. To address an indeterminate and anonymous audience of readers is very different from talking to visible students. It is not a conversation. One cannot take back in two minutes what one has already said, so the level of clarity has to be higher and there is no room for spontaneity. One means to say something that has not been said before and present it in a way suited to one's peers. Still one is teaching political theory, because in one way or another, one writes to instruct one's readers. The greatest difference in writing rather than talking is that one can concentrate entirely on getting it right. In that respect it is more like teaching graduate students, who, one hopes, will be the political theorists of the future. Because they are colleagues-in-the-making they force the teacher to acts of self-clarification and self-education at the highest level. That is what happens when one writes about any aspect of political theory as well, whether it be placing texts in historical context, a conceptual analysis, an explication of a text, or an argument about a set of ancient issues in the light of current experience. Not to do this at all is to doom oneself to intellectual stagnation and a sort of aged infancy, which cannot but damage one's performance as a direct teacher. And staleness, of course, sets an awful example to graduate students. The issue thus cannot be whether to teach or to write, but how to engage in two ways of teaching simultaneously or alternatively.

Some teachers can successfully write up and publish their lectures. Some of my most distinguished colleagues have written some of the best books this way. They think them through on their feet and then transform them into readable prose. For them the distinction between direct and indirect teaching hardly exists, and they often are the most accomplished and interesting lecturers. If they do anything indifferently it is the seminar and tutorial, simply because their strength is public presentation, in speech as well as in print. I, however, like many other scholars, must keep the two kinds of teaching completely apart. If I do not, my lectures become well-turned little essays and are hard to follow. Moreover, my better lectures, which do serve the needs of undergraduates, no longer seem to me fit for publication after I have given them. Writing up my lectures would strike me as simply warming up an uninteresting soup. What I like doing most, and probably do best, is small-group instruction. I enjoy teaching seminars for both undergraduate and graduate students. Ten to twenty people around a table, week after week, soon work together in an easy way, and though there should be a tense and even competitive spirit afoot, a lot can be achieved in discussing a single text in a group. Political theory lends itself particularly well to such teaching because it is naturally and inherently controversial. The best texts, however, do provide a core of inner unity, so the discussions do not fly all over the place. I find such instruction difficult but very rewarding when it goes well, though painful when it does not work out. In some mysterious way I also get ideas for articles and books out of these sessions.

Even devoted teachers have long periods of doldrums. What to do? Because political theory as a subject is always in motion, given its responsiveness to events, one cannot remain idle. Getting on with something new is important even before routine has made teaching a chore. Even going to a good conference a couple of times a year should be seen as a way of recharging the batteries. Is book reviewing a total waste of time? Not if one picks the books carefully. It is as good a way as any to keep up with the field. To escape from tedium one might avoid teaching the same courses too often or repeat them only every second year. Students can always be told in advance and can plan accordingly. They will be the beneficiaries of revised notes, rethinking, and an altogether livelier teacher. Teaching in a university quite unlike one's own can also be very invigorating. Absence notoriously inspires fondness. In any case something must be done. The worst thing that can happen to a teacher is just to rot away.

The importance of remaining actively engaged with political theory, by writing about it oneself and reading what others write, is particularly great when teaching graduate students. Talking to them about one's own writing is the best way of showing them how an article or a book is actually put together. Moreover, they help with their aggressive critical attitudes and with the generational differences they bring to bear on any discussion. Nothing is better for teaching the really good graduate students than making them realize that their ideas matter and that soon they will be ready to teach and write independently. What neither they nor the undergraduates need is to consume information served to them by a passive teacher who is neither actively contributing to the literature of political theory nor interested in new work of any kind. Whatever teaching political theory may be, it cannot merely amount to the relaying of some body of accepted wisdom which requires nothing but transmission from teacher to student. An element of inconclusive struggling between young and old is a very necessary part of the process of graduate education especially, and it cannot occur unless the teacher is also creative as an author, with all that implies psychologically and intellectually. The awful alternative to teaching as enjoyment with others is the repetition of the same wretched anecdotes and the same stale doctrines year after year by a teacher who cannot offer a graduate student a genuine picture of what real thinking is like. That is the certain fate of the political theorist who never writes at all or even falis to write about a fair variety of topics.

Teaching political theory, like any profession, has its built-in hazards, and there is no point in pretending that they do not exist. Tedium, indifference, and stagnation are the typical afflictions of older teachers. They will not be fatal if the instructor really feels an unabated passion for political thinking, for she can easily protect herself against the onset of a passing ill humor. If, however, she has really ceased to care about the subject, then there is no chance of recovery.

Indifference is not the only way to fail to teach honestly. The other extreme is also tempting and fatal in its own way. There is always a big demand for the guru-teacher at any university. Many young people seek leaders, superior parents, inspiration, and above all the feelings of whole-hearted discipleship. Most of us, either for lack of talent or by following plain good sense, find it easy to resist this call to serve as a prophet, but not all do. Political theory, being so close to ideology, particularly attracts students looking for a guru-teacher, and teachers who have both strong personal convictions and better than average rhetorical powers may find the prospect of a devoted following irresistible. The "masters" are not doing those students a favor because they end up retarding their maturation and closing their minds to the rich variety of alternative views. That they are betraying the scholarly vocation might also be a consideration, but most of all the gurus have ceased to care for political theory;

they are basically interested in themselves, in *their* message, in *their* followers, and in *their* renown.

If there are many ways of being a bad teacher and also of losing interest in teaching, there are also many gratifications. Every student is a new challenge and it is a delight to see the young catch on to the difficult texts and ideas, especially if they began as virtual *tabulae rasae*. And while a bad seminar session is pure hell a good one is surely a treat. Among the pleasures of teaching graduate students is that one does not lose touch with the best ones. They soon become one's colleagues and friends, the ups and downs of apprenticeship and late adolescence long since mercifully forgotten. It is the experience of renewal, of keeping political theory alive, and changing. The same thing does not occur in one's relations with undergraduates, and that is undeniably one of the more unfortunate facts about teaching. One never can really know what impact, if any, one has had on the young people who take notes in one's lectures, come to tutorials regularly and talk to one during office hours. They are usually very bright. That does not alter the likelihood that in a few years they will neither remember nor care about what I or anyone else taught them. Our effect upon their development may be profound, because we see them during a very intense and significant period in their lives, but it is an unknowable and forgotten little piece of their life's experiences even while at college, not to mention in "the real world." Our specific contribution is fleeting and forgettable. Two years out of college your students will remember you, but not what you said or got them to read, even if you impressed them in some enduring way. The negligible and indirect bearing one's work has on students cannot but give one a sense of futility at times. The best way to cope with such feelings is to concentrate on the learning that does go on visibly, even if its future functions must remain obscure. I place my bet on the students' being altered for the better, though in unknowable ways, by my teaching. And who would not say that knowledge, however digested, is not better than ignorance? And ignorant is what the young would be and remain if we did not teach them. Basically it depends upon us whether the entire college career of a young woman or man is significant and improving or not. Do we actually have a right to act on any other assumptions?

Some of the afflictions that threaten teachers are not entirely within our control, but there is one that is wholly self-inflicted and also contemptible. That is what I call the new snobbery. The old snobbery was bad enough. It tended to be the special preserve of humanists, political theorists among them. Its chief components were racism, antisemitism, and a fawning preference for the sons of the rich and famous. Deeply unintellectual, it was sometimes perfectly compatible with the more traditional forms of scholarship and fine teaching for the happy few. It did little to prepare anyone for the actual world and it was morally repulsive, with implications that eventually became quite clear. There is little left of that, because in time it became strangling and threatened the intellectual prospects of any university and the advance of the human as well as physical sciences. It has now been replaced by a different virus. It tells the world that clever young women and men should not become unglamorous schoolteachers, but should use the university as a platform from which to impress the world of affairs, to affect the public at large, and to find wealth and fame through the certificates of expertise that a university appointment yields. They will, so to speak, be instructing the entire nation by their advice. Write for conspicuous publications, meet, consult, attend, make money, and get your name into the newspapers, they tell us. The young will certainly yearn to be seen with them, will complain of their all too frequent absences, and if they ever do get to hear a lecture by the celebrity-professor they will get nothing, and not even realize that they have been cheated. Teaching is openly looked down upon and despised in a manner not unlike the disdain that the hereditary nobility of Europe used to feel for manual labor and trade. Except, of course, that the new snob is supposed to be a teacher and has simply sold himself, very successfully, it must be said, as something else and better to a gullible public.

The consequences of the new snobbery for the life of the university are fairly serious. It embitters the relations between the old and the young, the tenured and the untenured, in a wholly destructive way. In an institution where there are many justifiable and functional differences of prestige and rank, according to distinction, accomplishment, and age, it is particularly unnecessary and damaging to add useless and destructive ones. The untenured faculty is forced not only to do all the teaching, but they must hear their seniors openly refuse to teach and make derisory remarks about the poor mediocrities and the junior faculty who do it all. And with the association of ideas being what it is, teaching, when it is identified entirely with the young and untenured, is regarded with a diffuse contempt. Its source is surely the uneasy hostility that many an aging male feels and displays for the young, whom at another level he may well fear as successors. That is in itself a recipe for ill feeling. To add to it, when promotion time comes around, teaching is suddenly taken into account, but because the university authorities still require some proof of teaching skill, not because it is universally valued.

Adding to the demoralization of the young teacher is the pathetic effort of his seniors to look like natural scientists without actually doing analogous or similar work, and a general attitude of looking down at the merely local scene. This is the self-hating fantasy of many humanists and social scientists, and it does no one any good at all. There is no proof, moreover, that in spite of much pompous talk about research projects, grants, and the like these people actually produce better work or even publish more than those who quietly teach in classes and in writing. Like the old snobbery, the new variety expresses a very deep loss of self-esteem. And that brings us back to the beginning: to teach without loving one's subject at all, or caring for it a lot less than for other gratifications, whether material or intangible, is neither easy nor satisfying. Moreover, those who are neither scholars nor teachers now present a real menace to any university and to education generally. That is why the response of those who really understand what teaching is all about must simply be real self-respect grounded in the knowledge that they alone constitute the real world of learning now.

Reading and Writing:
In the Academy and Beyond

GREGORY NAGY

Teaching the Ordeal
of Reading

To call reading an ordeal is not an insult to learning. It is rather a challenge to the one who is learning to read, to read truly. The word itself is a challenge. Besides the empirical usage, as when sociologists or cultural anthropologists, outsiders peering in, speak comfortably of a given ordeal as instituted in a given society, there is also the distinctly uncomfortable personal usage, as when we speak of undergoing our own ordeals in life. In both dimensions, the empirical and the personal, there is something ongoing, the process of judgment. In fact, the German cognate of the English "ordeal" is *Urteil,* that is, "judgment." The ordeal of a rite of passage, for example, or of any personal agony, is a trial by fire or by water, as it were.

In the literature that I teach, the poetry and prose of preClassical and Classical Greece, the analogous word is *agōn,* which means both the given institution in which conflict happens and the personal agony of the one who participates in that conflict. These institutional and personal dimensions are still visible in the English borrowings, "antagonism" and "agony."

A premier example of *agōn* as an institution is the public performance of poetry by the poet who composed it, with or without the participation of a singing and dancing ensemble called the *khoros,* or "chorus." By implication, the poet is com-

163

peting with other poets, predecessors and contemporaries, as he or she approaches the force-field of public performance. In the Sixth Paean of Pindar, that consummate master of choral lyric, *agōn* is the word that captures the occasion (line 60) as the poet's art enters the arena of competition at the Feast of Theoxenia in Delphi.

In the diction of Pindar and other ancient Greek lyric poets, other words, such as *ponos, kamatos,* and *āthlos,* also convey the agony of competition in the performance of the composition. Each has its own nuances, but they all have one thing in common: the poet's agony of competitive creativity in recreating tradition. The more I teach about this agony to my students, the more I see that their own recreation of this agony through reading becomes an agony in and of itself, a rite of passage required of those who approach the force-field of performance, however many steps removed, as the attentive audience of that performance.

The audience, that is, the reader who stands for the audience, is put to the test, is judged, by the medium itself. In the poetic traditions inherited by Pindar the medium calls itself *ainos,* a word that is near-impossible to translate. My working definition, distilled from many years of worrying about the *ainos* with my students, is "a code that bears one true message to those who are qualified and many false messages to those who are not." The *ainos* presupposes a restricted audience, qualified as (1) the *sophoi:* those who are "skilled" or "wise" in decoding the message encoded by the poet;[1] (2) the *agathoi:* those who are "noble" and thus ethically predisposed to understand the message encoded in the poetry;[2] (3) the *philoi:* those who are "near and dear" and thereby connected to the poet and to each other, so that the message that is encoded in the poetry may be transmitted to them and through them—communication through community.[3]

1. Pindar, *Isthmian* 2.12-13.
2. Pindar, *Pythian* 2.81-88; cf. further at the end of the same poem, lines 94-96; also *Pythian* 10.71-72, at the end of another poem.
3. For example, see (again) Pindar, *Pythian* 2.81-88. For a detailed examination of the word *philos* as a poetic measuring-device for what anthropologists call "the ascending scale of affection," see Gregory Nagy, *The Best of the*

The *ainos*—a code carrying the right message for those who are qualified and the wrong message or messages for those who are unqualified—is predicated on the ideology of the ideal audience, listening to an ideal performance of an ideal composition. But at the same time it is predicated on the reality of uncertainties in interaction between performer and audience in the context of the actual performance of a composition: the *ainos* is by its very character ambiguous, both difficult in its form and enigmatic in its content. As a difficult code, the *ainos* communicates like an "enigma"—to use an English word that was borrowed from and serves as a translation for the Greek *ainigma*, which in turn is a derivative of *ainos*.[4]

The ideology of the ideal audience can best be seen in the song of the Muses and Graces, a divine chorus that has come to celebrate the wedding of Kadmos, founder of Thebes. Their song and dance, as dramatized by the poetry of Theognis (verses 15-18), is represented as the speech-act that *is* the foundation of community itself.[5] The words of the goddesses are quoted directly: *"hótti kalòn phílon estí, tò d' ou kalón ou phílon estí"* (whatever is beautiful is *philon*, whatever is not beautiful is not *philon;* Theognis, 17). In such a context, the closest approximation of *philon* would be something like "near and dear," in the sense of "socially cohesive." Beauty itself is being judged here in terms of one question: what is socially cohesive, and what is not? The essence of beauty is based here on this distinction, and it is not coincidental that the bride of Kadmos, founder of the local community, is none other than *Harmoniā* (see Hesiod, *Theogony*, 937, 975). The word *harmoniā* conveys simultaneously the aesthetic integration of the song and the

---

Achaeans: *Concepts of the Hero in Archaic Greek Poetry* (Baltimore: The Johns Hopkins University Press, 1979) pp. 104-115.

4. Cf. pp. 94-95 of G. Nagy, "Ancient Greek Epic and Praise Poetry," *Oral Tradition in Literature: Interpretation in Context*, ed. J. M. Foley (Columbia, Mo.: University of Missouri Press, 1986), pp. 89-102.

5. The passage in question, Theognis 15-18, is a centerpiece in the chapter entitled "Theognis and Megara: A Poet's Vision of His City," which I wrote for a volume entitled *Theognis of Megara: Poetry and the Polis*, ed. T. J. Figueira and G. Nagy (Baltimore: The Johns Hopkins University Press, 1985), pp. 22-81.

social integration of the community. Again the dictum applies: *communication through community*.

The ideal audience, the ultimate community, is built by the agony of testing, of selecting the qualified from among the unqualified. Just as the community tests the poet, the poetry tests the community. To be qualified, the audience has to understand the true message, and the very notion of poetic truth, *alētheia*, goes back to the ritual ideology of trial by water, where the true man stays afloat while the false man goes under.[6]

The *ainos* is like a man in disguise, whose real identity has to be decoded. Such is the case of Odysseus when he returns to Ithaca after a long absence, disguising himself as a beggar and putting everyone in the community to the test: will anyone recognize the true king, the body politic, for what he really is? In this role as disguised king, Odysseus is explicitly characterized as a master of *ainos* (*Odyssey XIV*, 508).[7] Who, then, succeeds in recognizing Odysseus for what he really is? I can let my students read for themselves, and I need not go into details here. Suffice it to say that the characters who do recognize Odysseus are the *sophoi* or "wise," the *agathoi* or "noble," and the *philoi* or "near and dear." Students can especially appreciate the "nearness and dearness" that leads to the individual scenes of recognition by the retainer, the nurse, the son, the wife, the father, and even the faithful dog Argos.

In the *Poetics* (1452a30) Aristotle defines *anagnōrisis* or "recognition" as a progressive shift from ignorance toward understanding, matching a shift toward *philiā*, that is, "nearness and dearness." This definition is remarkably suited to the semantics of the Greek word for the notion of "reading," that is, *anagignōskō*, which means, fundamentally, "to recognize." It is also compatible with the semantics of "reading" in another classical language: the Latin word for "reading" is *legō*, which means, fundamentally, "to select."

What is needed today in the teaching of literature, says this teacher, is a return to the genuine worth of reading as a rite of

6. M. Detienne, *Les Maîtres de vérité dans la Grèce ancienne*, 2nd. ed. (Paris: Maspero, 1973), pp. 29-50.

7. Detailed commentary in Nagy, *The Best of the Achaeans*, pp. 234-237.

passage, an ordeal wherein true values are rediscovered in an ever-anxious yet creative process of ongoing selection. The truest value is in that very process, a dynamic questioning and affirmation of the self, which is alien to the passive notion of data that must be absorbed, "material" that must be ingested by the consumers of a high-priced commodity that some dare to represent as "education." The teacher must participate in the rite of passage, travel with the student along that ever-changing "road of words"—to use the expression of Herodotus—that has been traveled by so many pilgrims of earlier times. In an era when the worth of a teacher is routinely tested as a commodity by consumers, the teacher of literature must bring to life yet again the voice that speaks to the audience, ever testing, ever challenging. The consumers of today must not prevail, any more than those ancient consumers, the suitors of Penelope, who were literally eating the absent king out of house and home. As the king was being consumed, so too is the body politic.

I close with the ultimate act of selection in literature, which is for me the choice that Achilles makes between a safe homecoming and an early death that will give him a *kleos* or "glory" that is "unwilting" (*Iliad* IX, 413). Achilles chooses *kleos,* which means not just "glory" but *the glory conferred by poetry.* Here the hero of epic chooses an "unwilting" existence in epic over life itself. For us, he chooses to be read, to be selected. And for me the wonder of it all is that this choice will keep on being made with each new reading, as I look hopefully to return yet another year to teach yet another generation who blossom now, only to wilt hereafter. The choice itself, to read, must remain unwilting.

RICHARD MARIUS

Reflections on the
Freshman English Course

For more than a century now, the standard freshman writing course in most colleges and universities has doubled as an introduction to literature. Because students interpret literature in the papers they write for such courses, the experience serves also as an introduction to literary criticism. In fact, the only encounter most normal human beings have had with that protean thing called "literary criticism" has been freshman English, where they must write about literature.

By a strange paradox, such courses seldom include any models to show what literary criticism can be or to demonstrate various approaches students can take in writing about literature. Students can go through a year-long freshman writing course about literature without knowing that professional literary criticism exists. Many problems in teaching both literature and freshman composition are thrown into relief by this paradoxical state of affairs.

The paradox has evolved out of history, especially Harvard's history, so intertwined in the general history of freshman English. Harvard's third Boylston Professor of Rhetoric, Edward T. Channing, held the chair for thirty-two years between 1819 and 1851 and shifted the emphasis from classical rhetoric, with its emphasis on teaching young men to speak well, to literary

169

criticism.[1] Channing had his students write voluminously, and he graded all their papers himself, recognizing that the ability to write well counted for more than the ability to speak well in the new American Republic. His successor, Francis James Child, lectured on Chaucer and handed the teaching of rhetoric over to an assistant. When Child was offered a position at Johns Hopkins, Harvard, to keep him, made him its first Professor of English.[2]

In 1874 what had been rhetoric became English composition, a pallid course with an obscure content. The emphasis changed from teaching rhetorical forms to making students write correctly, according to accepted conventions, and the status of writing teachers plummeted with the fallen status of the discipline of rhetoric itself. Everybody knew the conventions, so anybody could teach composition. Textbooks based on classical rhetoric were shelved. The course that became English A turned to the study of literature both as a standard for student prose and as subject for student writing.[3]

Writing about literature supposedly gave student compositions a seriousness they had often lacked in the earlier part of the century, when the emphasis on rhetorical form reduced content to triviality. (Richard Ohmann quotes a paragraph from one of those earlier nineteenth-century student themes, one beginning with the sentence, "Insects generally must lead a truly jovial life.")[4]

Early student themes on literature presented biographical information about the author, the historical context of the work, and often its moral value. In so doing, student writers mimicked the critical mood of the age. Literature professors apparently came strangers and afraid to the academy, where it had been supposed that students should read literature on their own. Teaching modern literature—any literature that had been done within the previous two or three centuries—seemed vaguely

1. Edward P. J. Corbett, *Classical Rhetoric for the Modern Student* (New York: Oxford University Press, 1971), p. 625.

2. Corbett, *Classical Rhetoric,* p. 626.

3. Corbett, *Classical Rhetoric,* pp. 626-627.

4. Richard Ohmann, *English in America* (New York: Oxford University Press, 1976), p. 98.

remedial on the one hand, vaguely frivolous on the other. Classical literature was presumed to inculcate manners, judgment, morality, and (since it was written in Greek and Latin) discipline. But modern literature—especially fiction—bordered on entertainment, and aroused opposition from faculty and students alike. Young Alvin M. Pappenheimer, Harvard class of 1899, observed, in a theme called "The Choice of Books" written for English A, that young men should choose their reading according to their own tastes. But, he concluded:

I have spoken above chiefly with reference to serious and educational works. As regards works of fiction, I wish to speak chiefly of their pernicious influence when interspersed between the reading of serious works. The resulting effect is similar to the distracting influence which we feel if we return from the theatre or some other place of amusement and then endeavor to solve some difficult problem requiring close and concentrated attention. For this reason, novel reading, breaking in as it does upon our regular work, seems to me to be by no means advisable.

By the next year, when Pappenheimer was a sophomore, he suggested that children be taught rhymes of useful content rather than meaningless jingles. Far better, he thought, to teach children that in "Fourteen Hundred and ninety-two, Columbus sailed the ocean blue" than the nonsense verse, "Hy diddle-diddle, the cat and the fiddle." It is pleasant to report that before he graduated, he was writing with appreciation about the seventeenth-century French poet Paul Scarron.

It looks as if the teaching of modern literature within the university became respectable because it supposedly civilized young men and women. So the enterprises of both literature and composition were sicklied over with a pale cast of banality. Professor Barrett Wendell, a man of considerable influence in the evolution of Harvard's English department, gathered his lectures on Shakespeare (he preferred the spelling "Shakspere") together in a little book that went through many editions. In it we find gems such as this passage on Shylock:

Shylock, like everybody else in the play, is presented as a human being. Distorted though his nature be by years of individual contempt and centuries of racial persecution, he remains a man. With the exception of his first "aside" in the presence of Antonio, there is nothing to prevent us from taking the proposal of the monstrous bond as something like a jest on his own usurious practices; and for all his racial hatred, he seems like many modern Hebrews, anxious for decent and familiar treatment by the people among whom he lives. The treatment he receives from the very Christians he has obliged, who apparently decoy him to supper that his daughter may have a chance for her thievish escapade, naturally arouses all the evil in him. His revenge, if not admirable, is most comprehensible. Not so, to modern feeling, is the contemptuously brutal treatment which he receives from the charming people with whom we are expected to sympathize fully.[5]

Here is literature used as a sort of pulpit from which its practitioner offers some vague and comfortable moralisms about the human condition with a nod in the direction of the doctrine of progress. Wendell's view of literature corresponded remarkably to the view of religion held by his contemporary Phillips Brooks and other princes of the pulpit among American Protestants. Both granted a certain solace to those upper middle-class Americans who, having abandoned the crudities of frontier religion and facing extreme challenges to their sensibilities by waves of non-Anglo-Saxon immigration and other sea changes in society, needed some assurance that their own culture and values were founded in a durable tradition. I suspect that the development of courses in Shakespeare and Chaucer had some affinities to the increasing pride some Americans felt in tracing their ancestry to the Mayflower or to the Cavaliers of Virginia. Both affirmed the moral and cultural superiority of English language and English ways over the motley and polyglot swarms of arrivals from the Continent. The turn of the English composition course towards "correct English" enforced the same tendencies. Wendell looks like the cynosure of an educated Anglo-Saxon middle-class impulse. A knowledge of literature created an eminence of understanding whence one might look at a moiling world with a certain detachment and superiority.

Wendell also published a popular little book called *English Composition,* a collection of eight lectures given at the Lowell

5. Barrett Wendell, *William Shakspere* (New York: Charles Scribner's Sons, 1901), pp. 151-152.

Institute. Like his book on Shakespeare, *English Composition* passed through edition after edition, now reposing in unread files on the shelves of Widener Library.

He viewed composition as a rational and orderly process. Words were the foundation; words were combined into sentences; sentences were combined into paragraphs; and paragraphs were combined into essays. He devoted successive chapters to these steps, and added a chapter on elegance, making composition seem linear, progressive, and simple. How does one achieve elegance? By reading great authors—Marlowe, John Ford, Alexander Pope, and James Russell Lowell. He also commends the musical drama of Richard Wagner.

Here his work demonstrates amnesia toward classical rhetoric, for Wendell makes no sustained effort to analyze the elegance of the writers he lauds, almost certainly because he lacked the tools to make such an analysis. He probably read aloud to his students with some feeling, assuming (not entirely incorrectly) that if would-be writers were exposed to great literature, they would absorb elegance by a sort of intellectual osmosis. They would also absorb the proper values. "If we are writing stories in which we wish the reader's sympathy to go with our characters," Wendell wrote, "we should be careful not to make the characters do anything disgusting."[6] Among the disgusting habits he mentioned was picking one's teeth in public. It sounds as if Wendell thought that one's characters should not do anything that would not get them invited back to the right homes. And it seems that the chief value he placed on knowing literature was its ability to enable one to be at home with the right sort of people.

The notion that writing about literature should teach gentility and moral lessons and dwell on biography has long since died. Literary criticism has become a discipline taught in universities, an Atlas holding up the skies of the Modern Language Association, and an enormous academic enterprise. Recent criticism has illuminated not only individual works, modes, and authors, but also the way we think about any text, whether it be fiction,

6. Barrett Wendell, *English Composition* (New York: Charles Scribner's Sons, 1907), p. 294.

poetry, drama, the essay, or a historical source. The rudiments of modern critical theory resemble some loss of innocence that can never be restored; after a bite of those ideas, no text appears quite certain, no interpretation final, no meaning entirely clear.

In the last two decades, the study of English composition has enjoyed a parallel flourishing. Rhetoric has revived after its long sleep. The Conference on College Composition and Communication gathers over four thousand writing teachers for its annual meeting in mid-March, rivaling the English literature sections of the MLA in its vigor and numbers.

The simultaneous recovery of rhetoric and rise of Structuralist and Post-Structuralist criticism are perhaps not merely coincidental phenomena. Both are intensely psychological. Both involve concentrated attention to the way we perceive "reality" by means of words, both express a skepticism about the power of "reality" of itself to impose itself on the human mind without the mediation of fluid and suspect codes. Both pay great attention to the active role of the audience in creating a piece of writing.

It is a bit ironic that rhetoric has long had a bad name on account of a general perception that its forms are not necessarily related to truth, while modern criticism has attained academic deification for pointing out the many difficulties to the process of grasping truth through any text. But so be it. More ironic is the separation and mutual suspicion—even hostility—existing between the two disciplines, a state of affairs that extends to the freshman English course that, in most colleges and universities, doubles as a literature course. Here our paradox rises like a cordilleran spine. What part of the energetic intellectual activity of modern criticism gets into the composition *cum* literature course? What part does some rudimentary understanding of rhetoric play in helping students understand literature? The answer to both questions is the same: Precious little.

The textbooks illustrate the issue. In many introductory literature courses in American universities, students are presented with an anthology in one or two thick volumes, filled with short stories, poetry, plays, and occasionally essays from the long history of literature—sometimes English and American, sometimes only one or the other, sometimes with selections from the literature of other languages thrown in. These anthologies are usually assigned to classes along with an English handbook, a work intended as a reference for issues as diverse as the writing process, correct punctuation, and the rules of grammar. Publishers tell me that these anthologies do extraordinarily well in the academic marketplace.

A teacher assigns a paper on, say, William Faulkner's "A Rose for Emily" or Flannery O'Connor's "Everything That Rises Must Converge" (two stories bound to appear in every anthology). There may be twenty-five or thirty students in a class; a hard-pressed teacher has little opportunity to comment at length on every paper. But she can memorize the handbook, mark errors on the papers, and refer the students to the places in the handbook where those errors are discussed.

I know of no anthology intended for classroom use that includes critical essays by professionals on the literature that students are reading. Many anthologies include summary introductions to the various parts of the books. Sometimes these are splendid. But none of these prefatory essays is the sort of writing students will be doing once they use the anthology in the freshman English class.

The hidden assumption here bears examination. In journalism school, aspiring newspaper reporters read news stories, feature articles, and editorials and learn by those models how to write similar things. In economics, in history, in every other discipline in the humanities, students read professional books and articles about subjects in the discipline, and seek to imitate them. Source books that include primary and secondary material abound in these disciplines. The history teacher has a choice of dozens of collections of important articles by historians about this or that issue in the discovery of the past. History students read primary sources, but they also read secondary sources that resemble in methodology and appearance the writing that the students are supposed to do.[7]

7. The *appearance* of a model piece of writing is extraordinarily important in helping students understand what sort of writing is to be required of them. Students who read scholarly articles or books that have footnotes or endnotes as well as bibliographies learn almost unconsciously that form is extremely

Only in the traditional freshman course in literature are students customarily presented with one kind of writing—fiction, poetry, plays—and told to write something different in intention, methodology, and appearance. Teachers lead students in classroom discussion of literature, and they require students to write papers about that literature. For many decades, the only requirement of those papers was that they observe the grammatical conventions, that they be "correct" or embody what Barrett Wendell called "good use." But a completely correct essay can also be utterly mindless. With the advent of the new rhetoric over the past two decades, the teaching of composition in colleges has been changing. But the discrepancy between the forms of literature students *read* and the forms of essays that they *write* long ago became glaring and remains so.

Teachers may ignore critical literature because they assume that a lively classroom discussion of literature should by itself generate essays that apply the critical principles learned in good talk. An appropriate analogy would be the belief that talking about baseball makes one a good hitter without the necessity of playing the game. Yet the differences between writing and speaking are implacable. Discussion of literature does not *ipso facto* lead to perceptive writing about literature. So, year after year, freshman papers do little more than summarize the plot or give us three reasons for believing that ambition is a theme in *Macbeth*. And year after year teachers in such courses read those papers, berate themselves for not being better teachers, berate their students for not writing better papers, and, worst of all, assume that they must lower the level of their teaching to the evident incapacity of their students.

The triviality of composition papers about literature is surely one of the reasons for the low status of those people who teach required writing courses in universities. *Real* faculty members

---

important in making members of the community of discourse represented by the discipline in question take a piece of writing seriously. A friend of mine in economics once observed to me that students can often make their papers *look* like economics papers even when they do not *read* like true economics papers. My response was that teaching them the form of an economics paper was probably indispensably primary to teaching them how to write a true essay in economics.

like to think that they can graduate from such stuff, that they can ascend to a more ethereal world of teaching where the ideas are the thing—especially their own ideas. Student writing in these advanced classes can then be relegated to a term paper or to perhaps a few short essays to be read by a graduate assistant. No Boylston Professor of Rhetoric at Harvard has taught freshman composition for almost a century. The teaching of freshman English *cum* composition has been left to the young and the untenured or to those tenured professors who, having published little or nothing, land in freshman English as punishment for their sins of academic omission. In many schools, freshman English has become a dusty arena stained with the blood of unwilling martyrs to lost faiths—the lost faith of teachers in their students and the lost faith of students in themselves and the capacity of literature to speak to them.

The difficulties students have in writing about literature are not limited to the freshman course. As a reader of senior honors theses in English, I am discouraged by how often our students announce a topic—perhaps some idea that they find in the text of their chosen author—and proceed to discuss that topic by means of commentary attached to a plot summary, the supposed argument carried on *seriatim* without any organizing principle: "Look, here in the beginning we find ambition in Macbeth when he meets the three witches. Look, here is ambition again when he writes to Lady Macbeth. Look, here it is again when they talk." We are walked through the paper as though we might be walked through an art gallery, our guide pointing out the various sights in a commentary shaped by the physical arrangement of the paintings. Many student writers surrender haplessly to the physical arrangement of the literary texts they are examining. The result is plot summary. Plot summary is almost fated to lose both writer and reader in a mass of details where the connecting thread becomes a rope of sand.

Most students cannot define a literary argument that they can expound without this plodding march to detach themselves from the form of the text itself and to arrive at a different form, the form of a critical essay with its own beginning, middle, and end distinct from the beginning, middle, and end of the text they have chosen for their study. This bondage to the order of the text is in part created by general ignorance of the way seasoned critics approach texts.

Too many senior theses in English demonstrate little awareness of the critical literature that any important text generates around itself as scholars are drawn to it. In the spring of 1987, I read a senior thesis that purported to discuss three texts of immense historical significance to English literature. The student writer made passing reference to two or three general books about this material but then attacked the texts themselves with an almost touching innocence of the vast scholarship that had through the years defined and refined all the issues the student addressed. The consequence was a paper that made exclamatory discoveries of the obvious.

There is, of course, a place for the meticulous examination of a text without trucking in long lists of critical scholarship on the subject. But such authority comes out of profound knowledge of the literature itself, the criticism generated by the literature, and the tools of criticism. For mature scholars, knowledge of the critical literature provides the scaffolding that may then be removed from their own work as they write. Without the scaffolding, the scholars could not have constructed their own works. Our students, like apprentice carpenters, need to demonstrate that they can build the scaffold. But because they often remain innocent of the critical context of literary works, their own essays sometimes collapse into mush.

Why are freshmen and many other students as well not given critical models for the critical writing they are supposed to be doing? Why are critical essays not analyzed in the classroom with the same zeal devoted to the primary literature?

An obvious answer is that there is not enough time. Today's students have so little experience in literature that teachers feel compelled to stuff them as full of it as they can. This generation does not read, and it has not memorized poetry (even the bad poetry students of my generation routinely memorized when we were children), or biblical texts, or passages from Shakespeare, or historical documents such as the Gettysburg Address or the Declaration of Independence. Consequently they are strangers not only to those points of reference that might help them navigate the literary sea, but also to the underlying cadences that have governed the development of written English. They cannot write because they have not read and they cannot hear.

Not long ago, Jerry Doolittle, a former presidential speech writer and now a teacher on my staff in Expository Writing Program, gave his students a whimsical quiz. They were supposed to fill in the blanks for twenty statements including the following:

I think that I shall never see a poem lovely _____ (three words)

You're a better man than I am _____ (two words)

Good fences make _____ (two words)

In Xanadu did _____ (two words)

I met a traveler from an antique _____ (one word)

Water, water, every where, nor any drop _____ (two words)

Quoth the raven, _____ (one word)

A jug of wine, a loaf of bread and _____ (one word)

The class comprised fifteen students. The average score for the twenty questions was seven, a score somewhat elevated, so Doolittle tells me, because everyone in the class correctly filled in the blanks for "Winston tastes good, like a _____ (two words)" and "This Bud's for _____ (one word)."

We are engaged, I think, for the first time in our cultural history, in teaching students how to write without assuming that they have learned how to read. The authority of the written language has declined. I am not here lamenting a decline in the *quality* of language. I am arguing that the relative unfamiliarity of our students with literature or with reading itself makes it extremely difficult to teach them certain things that we have often taken for granted. The issue goes beyond content. True, they do not possess a common body of literary knowledge. They do not recognize biblical allusions. They do not know classical mythology. The do not know Shakespeare. They have not memorized poetry. But more important, they have not absorbed certain literary forms that earlier students—Barrett Wendell's certainly—knew even if they did not know they knew them.

They have a hard time making a linear exposition because

they have not read expositions that begin by assuming that the writer and readers agree that A is true, then argues that if A is true, B must also be true, and that if A and B are true, C must also be true. They have a hard time constructing a narrative because they have not read many narratives. They cannot pick arguments out of literature or make arguments of their own because they have not pored over literature enough to recognize that it has an argument.

This last is an especially critical deficiency. Every good piece of prose, whether fiction or nonfiction, and most poetry has its argument. The argument embodies premises and statements that support conclusions directly stated or indirectly implied. The argument of a text allows us to understand why a text has its particular form. The ability to recognize the argument allows us to summarize the text and to talk or write about it intelligently. We learn to write, in part, by reading and by appropriating a sort of internal canon that tells us when an argument is present and when it is not. That is to say that, in reading, we learn not only words and their meanings but to recognize ways of putting those words together to make the argument appropriate to the mode the writer has chosen.

The bond between the writing teacher and an internalized literary canon in student audiences scarcely exists any more. So the teacher of the standard freshman writing *cum* literature course has reasons for keeping it simple. Why complicate things by bringing in the literature of criticism? Why not stuff our charges with as many of the primary texts as we can in the time we have? Maybe something will stay down. Maybe someone will start reading to see how the stories turn out. We might even get student poets to read some poems. Why not stay with the traditional humanist approach that involves reading the text and pointing out details that students might have missed, perhaps adding some comments about the relevance of the literature to the general human condition? *Macbeth is* about ambition, and it has some great lines that illuminate common human feelings. Barrett Wendells' criticism of Shakespeare involved a continual presentism, a demonstration that literature could speak directly to our situation, that it is not dead. Why not tell them that Shylock is a human being, showing that human beings are always the same in every age and that knowing Shylock helps us to know our own time? True, such an approach is likely to make us comfortable in our own prejudices by sanctifying them with the anointing of tradition. And student papers from such teaching are usually banal. But are those sufficient reasons to make us shift the ground of our teaching?

Yes they are. The current mood seems to be that we will take anything students give us because we do not expect students to give us much. They do not give us much because they recognize, however unconsciously, our expectations, and they descend to meet them.

They also do not give us much because they have no clear idea of how to give us something substantial. They lack models that might open, simultaneously, questions they can ask about literature and rhetorical forms of criticism that might allow them to speculate about possible answers to those questions. A teacher's random commentary on this or that interesting facet of a text leads to the sort of confusion created by a teacher who marks every conceivable error on a paper without ever pointing out to the student writer that errors fall into patterns, and that discovery of the patterns is the prior requirement for correcting the individual mistakes. I think that students know that when they write banal papers. It may be the dull, throbbing knowledge of an unlocalized pain, but they know. And it effectively prevents many students from enjoying the experience that literature is supposed to inspire.

We may adduce a further pedagogical reason for avoiding the literature of criticism in our freshman courses. College students, especially freshmen, seldom believe that their own considered judgments are worth anything. They may assert their opinions vehemently: "In my opinion, Antigone was totally wrong because she broke the law, and you can't go around breaking the law." But such writing represents an abdication of considered judgment. It sets up opinion as a sort of religious creed beyond contradiction. Its frequent iteration in student papers is a reflection of the uncertainty students feel in building an interpretative argument from texts.

Many teachers of freshman composition, aware of the disbelief of students in their own mental processes, think that if students read, say, Peter Brooks on Joseph Conrad's *Heart of Darkness,* they will be unable to write about Conrad's work themselves. They will be paralyzed by all that Brooks sees in the story, and they cannot then see anything in it on their own. Worse, they may turn to plagiarism, feeling that since they must write something about the story and that Brooks has written all there is to write on the subject, they must copy out what Brooks has said and present it as their own work. Writing teachers must always do battle with plagiarism; Howard Mumford Jones delighted in telling of the summer-school student who once presented to him as her own an essay that he had written himself. I have talked with many freshman English teachers who on principle refuse to assign literary criticism because they fear to stultify student minds or to encourage dishonesty.

But were the academy at large to react in a similar way to such fears, the use of any secondary sources would be impossible. Teachers of history, of astronomy, of biology, of chemistry, of philosophy, of religion all require their students to use secondary sources in writing papers within those disciplines. Why should freshman English be different?

Perhaps another reason for avoiding the literature of criticism in the freshman lit. course is that the quality of writing in such work is seldom a model of style to be imitated, especially the writing of Structuralist and Post-Structuralist critics. I have often observed that the old canard that knowledge of Latin and Greek somehow helps one write English well is amply refuted by an examination of the various journals in classics published in this country and in England. One might plausibly argue also that much of the writing in journals devoted to literary criticism refutes the notion that English departments are the proper custodians of language.

Only critics read other critics. An obvious reason for this state of affairs is that to understand criticism, one has to have read the work being criticized—making the reading of literary criticism a special sort of intellectual task. But something more is at issue. Most lay people who read literature do not read criticism. A noted critic observed somewhat sorrowfully in my presence several years ago that although one may walk into a lawyer's office and see novels and poetry on the shelves, one never sees works of literary criticism except on the shelves of literary critics. Now and then trade publishers will bring out a particularly outstanding piece of literary criticism, but the outlet for most literary criticism is the university press, and even there it is far down the list—almost at the bottom, so editors at university presses tell me—of things that sell. I must admit to being seldom swept up into the conviction that I am in the hands of a critic who is also master of the words and cadences. Sometimes I do not even know what I am reading.

Why is literary criticism generally unread and frequently unreadable? Is the subject itself intrinsically interesting only to certain kinds of minds? Is some molecular biologist likely to discover a longish arm on one side of a gene, predisposing the bearer to literary criticism in the way that others are to music or manic depression? Or is it that critics have given up on their own language because they have almost unconsciously lost hope for their discipline to influence anything? Ludwig Wittgenstein once ran into his friend F. R. Leavis and demanded that Leavis stop being a critic. Terry Eagleton speculates that "perhaps Wittgenstein thought that Leavis should give up literary criticism because, like philosophy, it changed nothing."[8]

It may be that the inaccessibility (to put it charitably) of much critical prose arises from a lack of confidence or expectation among critics themselves. It might be argued that writers are motivated to write well and to polish their prose in proportion to their expectation of being widely read. Such a notion does not contradict Flaubert's comment to a friend, "One must write for one's self above all; it is the only way to write well." Flaubert could scarcely have worked so hard unless he had assumed a world of similar selves out there, waiting to read what he wrote for himself. Many modern critics seem to have abandoned just that expectation. True, some aspects of literary criticism are intrinsically difficult, and as Richard Lanham has observed in his typically vigorous way, clarity can be "a disastrous criterion for prose style."[9] Yet we must ask ourselves if so much work

8. Terry Eagleton, *Against the Grain* (London: Verso, 1986), p. 100.
9. Richard A. Lanham, *Style: An Anti-Textbook* (New Haven: Yale University Press, 1974), p. 37.

in literary criticism must be as obscure and as miserably written as it is.

A great many teachers of literature nowadays believe profoundly that some modern critical schools are positively pernicious. Some extremes of Structuralist criticism, for example, might well seem to traditional humanist critics to turn the joys of literature into mud—well blocked, carefully arranged mud, but mud nevertheless. Having slogged through most of Jacques Derrida's *De la Grammatologie* (Paris, Editions de Minuit, 1967), I would be reluctant to inflict on students, especially beginning students, some of those concepts and much of that prose, even in the best translations. Many of Derrida's American disciples have fallen onto a jargon that makes us believe readily in codes because their critical essays must be painfully and laboriously deciphered. One may argue, as Robert Scholes has, that the very effort of some critics such as Saussure to turn criticism into an exact science has led their work to unbearable extremes.[10] It has made them thoroughly unscientific. I suspect that many of these critics have composed a jargon that, like all jargon, imposes on its users the illusion of clarity and precision while in fact leading them to confusion and opacity.

Yet there is literate, accessible criticism. The disjunction between criticism by professional critics and criticism by the beginning student is perhaps not a calamity, but as I said early in this essay, it is a paradox. For many of the insights of modern criticism should help the teacher charged with teaching both writing and literature in the same course, and an acquaintance on the part of the students with some of these issues might cause them to see their own writing in a different light. I would not be so innocent as to argue that reading and carefully interpreting a few critical essays can work a revolution in students' understanding of literature. But I do believe that we impoverish ourselves and our teaching by the divorce between literature and criticism that seems evident in the anthologies, and that I take to be common in most introductory courses.

What is to be done? I believe that every literature course

10. Robert Scholes, *Textual Power* (New Haven: Yale University Press, 1985), pp. 96-97.

should include some detailed, analytical attention to the literature of criticism. That is, critical essays on literature should be discussed in class with the same attention that we have traditionally given to the discussion of plays, short stories, novels, and poetry. The rhetoric of the critical essay should be studied as thoroughly as the rhetoric of fiction, poetry, and drama. What does this writer say? What does the writer say that has implications beyond the text that is the subject of the critical essay? What inferences does this writer make? How is this writer reading the text? How does the argument progress in this essay? What are the dominant words? What sentences encapsulate the whole? What does the writer assume that we know? How well does the thesis of this essay correspond to what you read in the text the writer is discussing?

I would not go so far as to suggest that every primary text assigned in the course should be joined to a secondary critical text. Coverage is a false god but still too venerated among teachers of literature for such a radical proposal to be taken seriously by most of them. We should have more anthologies like the one done by the later Oscar Williams,[11] which comprised one hundred poems and essays on the poems by leading critics of the time. At the very least some critical essays should break into the common anthologies.

No literature course should be taught without a strong writing component, and student papers should be compared to the critical writing that professional critics do. We apparently cannot do away with the large lecture course in literature. These usually have discussion sessions attached. These small group sections may be interesting and provocative. But almost anyone who has led a vigorous and fascinating discussion of literature is likely to experience shock, dismay, and perhaps humility in looking at the essays students produce following that discussion. Great lecturers might help themselves as well as their students if they regularly presided over at least one small section attached to their large classes, and if they read student writing and commented upon it—and perhaps changed their lectures to accom-

---

11. Oscar Williams, *Master Poems of the English Language* (New York: Washington Square Press, 1967).

modate what they learn of student understanding of what they say.

I have spent uncounted hours observing small classes where my teachers in Expository Writing have been at work with students. I have read innumerable papers that have come out of these classes. I am convinced that the only way to engage and test the minds of students is to have them write and write and write. But if they write, we should read their writing and comment on it for its ability to frame and sustain an argument, for the use of evidence, and for its capacity to define important issues concerning the text at hand. The thought processes of professional critics in essays about literature should be examined, and student essays should be measured for the presence of similar processes.

In particular student essays about literature should be examined for the inferences they make. Good criticism always involves an inferential leap from the bare text to the critic's view of what that text means, a leap immediately perceptible to careful readers. Without some self-conscious attention to the process of inference from literary text to interpretation, students may avoid inference altogether (plot summary again) or else they may infer wildly and without a sense of the difference between plausible and implausible interpretations.

Students should also have the opportunity to revise their papers in consequence of the teacher's commentary on them, and the emphasis on the revision should be much more on form and content than on style. Students discover style as they discover that they have something interesting to say only by being taught the shape of the essay and its well-nigh implacable requirements.

Part of the writing students do should be about criticism. We have discovered that students in Expository Writing love to do research papers where they have a body of evidence to study and some choice in what they will write about. Many of our teachers have enjoyed great success by having students do research papers of eight or ten pages on the critical response to various works of literature. What have the critics said? What different things have various critics seen in the texts? How does this or that critical approach determine the way a critic looks at a text? How does the critical response to a book change over the years? Students often need help in limiting the argument of such papers to manageable size. But it can be done; we regularly do it.

Some attention should be given in the teaching of literature to certain issues now lively in various critical schools. The most important, I think, would be the modern skepticism about the power of language to communicate, the sense that whatever it communicates is a consequence of shared experience between writer (or speaker) and audience, the realization that no experience is entirely shared and that consequently no language can communicate to an audience precisely what a writer intends. As I mentioned above, the place of the audience in modern criticism corresponds in many ways to the attention to concepts of audience provided by the new rhetoric. Here is a place where the two fields can come together.

The idea of the difficulty of language is not new to Structuralist and Post-Structuralist critics, and it may be examined without their sometimes appalling jargon. Sometimes it can be addressed within a historical context providing insight into the origins of such skepticism. Surely the skepticism arises in part from the radical breakdown of comity in many modern political movements, where political foes make radically different readings of the same texts and the same events. The idea of the loyal opposition rests on some agreement about fundamental texts, and if that agreement is absent, democracy itself becomes impossible as political foes become lethal enemies all in the name of correct definitions.

It cannot be accidental that one of the most cogent expressions of the difficulties of text is to be found in the "Prólogo para Franceses"[12] by José Ortega y Gasset, written at a moment when the idea of comity was dissolving throughout Europe. Ortega spoke of the original essays, written in 1926 "for a certain number of Spaniards whom destiny had placed before me," and pondered the difficulties of communicating these articles several years later to a French audience. At best, he said, we say only

---

12. José Ortega y Gasset, in his *La Rebelión de las Masas*, 13th ed. (Madrid: Espasa-Calpe, 1956).

a part of what we think and place an unbridgeable gulf before the transmission of the rest.[13] We do not speak *urbi et orbi*, he wrote, unless we say nothing.[14] We speak particularly—to a particular time and a particular place. His book had become popular in other lands, he said, only because of the "terrifying homogeneity of situations into which the entire Occident is sinking."[15] Only a common experience offered any possible matrix for the common apprehension of language, and even then that common apprehension was incomplete, sometimes calamitously incomplete.

Ortega did not venture off into the extreme view that communication is impossible. *Something* is communicated in every act of speaking and writing within a given community of discourse. Something must be communicated in general through a society, or politics becomes impossible. But students are usually unaware of how much of their own experience they read into any text and how, consequently, just as Carl Becker once declared that every man is his own historian (and woman, too, we might add), so is every reader his (or her) own writer, never apprehending the naked words of the author, but adding to the words the experiences the words are supposed to signify and the previous experience of the reader with the words themselves, experiences inevitably different from the experiences of the author. It may be argued that an understanding of this issue is fundamental to modern political discourse and to the comity that allows democracy to endure.

But here my aim is the lower one of making our students take more care in writing their own language by showing them how difficult the business of communication is, and making them appreciate more that which literature does communicate despite all the difficulties. Our students still think of language as a transparent screen through which they see the reality the language is supposed to represent. They cannot unlearn this illusion by random notations of this or that detail that their own experience has not prepared them to see. All writing intended for an audience begins with drawing a circle of assumed shared

13. Ortega y Gasset, *La Rebelión,* p. 10.
14. Ortega y Gasset, *La Rebelión,* p. 11.
15. Ortega y Gasset, *La Rebelión,* p. 12.

experience and knowledge around the writer and readers. From that circle, writers move to what they have experienced beyond the common sharing, and they seek to draw readers along this new ground. To a large degree, the writer creates an audience in the opening lines of the writing. Just what is shared turns out to be much more delicate, much more fragile than most students suspect. I do not believe we are teaching literature until we are showing them just how fragile that sharing is.

A literature course should also consider the nature of narrative. Our students do reasonably well in writing stories about themselves, especially if they can consider themselves victims of this or that oppression or injustice; they have immense difficulty in constructing narratives about events outside themselves. Yet in almost any literature course they encounter narratives on every hand. Do they understand how narratives work? Probably not.

Narrative, I think, is the foundation of all literature and all writing. By understanding the form of narrative, its conventions, its necessities, its assumptions of what is shared between writer and reader, its sense of what is shared by the silences of the author, its general shape and its various forms, we learn something about the nature of writing and perhaps the nature of the human mind. That understanding is not automatic. We come to it either by hearing or reading stories all our lives or by having it explained carefully to us by teachers, critics, and rhetoricians and then by putting that understanding to work in writing narratives of our own and in figuring out the narrative structure in what we read.

My point is not to argue in detail about the problems of language or the nature of narrative. These are matters under intense discussion among literary critics and rhetoricians, and I think they should be discussed in the course we usually call freshman English and in other literature courses as well. My main argument is that the literature of criticism and of rhetoric is part of general English literature. Despite the reluctance of freshman English teachers to analyze criticism, we should undertake the task.

Little endures in the students' minds out of piecemeal discussion of fiction, drama, and poetry. The principles that inform that discussion can endure. A huge body of work is devoted to these principles, and we should teach enough of it so that students can better apprehend what literature and the study of literature are. Students should read the literature of criticism as they read the works the criticism considers. They should study the form of criticism, examine its assumptions and its evidence, judge its style, and weigh it for that impalpable thing called truth.

If we should take my suggestions seriously, we would have to subject to immense scrutiny the content of our lectures and discussions, the kind of writing assignments we make in the freshman English course, and the assumptions we make about the purposes of the entire enterprise of teaching both literature and writing in college. It seems at least worthwhile at this moment of ferment in higher education to take stock.

JAMES ENGELL

Eroding the Conditions
for Literary Study

Where literary texts are systematically taught and where teaching itself receives intense scrutiny—the college or university—is not always where literature is either learned or loved most. But instead of improving, the conditions for teaching, learning, and above all for loving literature are deteriorating in many present academic settings, particularly in institutions of higher learning pressed for space, enmeshed in urban environments that have become restrictive, reliant on faculty increasingly composed of commuters, dependent on outside funds overwhelmingly tied to the natural and social sciences, and squeezed for student housing to the extent that Virginia Woolf's minimal condition for productive literary activity, "a room of one's own," is now denied to most women and men alike, and instead allotted to the rich, the lucky, or seniors in their second term. In short, the changing physical and temporal environment of the American university and of many colleges is, for purposes of teaching and studying literature, changing for the worse.

The effect of this subtle but far-reaching change can only be negative and cannot be underestimated. As college populations increase and admissions applications set record highs at many schools year after year, not only has the study of literature changed—it always will, just as it always has—and not only have new questions been raised and new critical methods been created, but something unprecedented, usually glossed over, has developed: a decline in the conditions provided for literary study.

And by "conditions" I do not mean conditions of the faculty— leave time, schedules, tenure decisions, course loads, compensation, grants and fellowships, or support staff. These play a crucial role in the quality of teaching and scholarship, but they also receive constant attention and lobbying. Nor do I mean the more general sociological conditions of literature in what Northrop Frye calls our "post-literate" age, a society barraged with visual images and one not widely composed of avid readers: almost half of American adolescents now attend college, yet one quarter of the adult population is functionally illiterate and a larger percentage fails to achieve what E. D. Hirsch indentifies as "cultural literacy."

Rather, my topic here is the conditions of literary study for students in day-to-day college life. Every serious student, eager to learn, curious and devoted, with whom I speak, is concerned about literary study not only in the classroom but outside as well, where, after all, most of our time is spent and where we do virtually all our reading, writing, and much or most of our talking about literature. These conditions might be characterized under several headings: a room of one's own (privacy), secure blocks of time without hourly pressures, deadlines, or activities, well-run and well-designed libraries, and the opportunity and comfortable space for conversation with faculty and peers.

Students, whatever their individual literary interests, likes and dislikes, or opinions of specific instructors or methods, agree that they rarely enjoy the privacy and undisturbed time to read and digest a significant body of literature, to agonize over texts whose reward is in direct proportion to the hours spent on them, or to write and rewrite with the care they wish to exercise. Even contrasted with the atmosphere in which I began teaching only fifteen years ago, it seems that fewer students are now able "to find the time" to read books not specifically assigned in courses. Yet most teachers swear that reading lists are shorter today than a generation ago. Before blaming secondary schools, the stereo amplifier, economic facts of life, or the students' own bad planning, we might examine the pressures that are eroding conditions favorable to the study and teaching of literature. Of course this problem is more pressing in some institutions than in others, and generally poses less of a threat to small, well-endowed liberal arts colleges. But when presidents of major research universities and MacArthur fellows in the humanities or qualitative social sciences complain that even they cannot do their own writing where they teach or work and cannot even devise their best ideas there, but must "get away" from the hectic pace, cramped quarters, cascade of events, lectures, schedules, activities, and vulnerability to interruption, we should listen to students who voice similar complaints. "Shakespeare's plays," writes Virginia Woolf in her famous essay *A Room of One's Own,* "seem to hang there complete by themselves. But when the web is pulled askew, hooked up at the edge, torn in the middle, one remembers that these webs are not spun in midair by incorporeal creatures, but are the work of suffering human beings, and are attached to grossly material things, like health and money and the houses we live in." Likewise, the study and love of those plays and of other works, too, seem attached to similar conditions.[1]

Students frequently do not have a room to call their own. We seem thrown back upon those conditions Woolf relates with irony and anger as she describes efforts to raise money for a woman's college. "We cannot have sofas and separate rooms. 'The amenities . . . will have to wait.' "[2] At present, many colleges, even comparatively wealthy ones, resort to housing "overflow" students in hotels or condos, putting two or three in one room. Less than sixty years ago, the House system at Harvard was designed not only to break the power of the clubs supported by wealthy undergraduates, but to provide for each student one room of his own. The latter motivation, in fact, acted as the guiding principle of House architectural design, which also provided extensive faculty office space in those Houses,

1. *A Room of One's Own* (New York and London: Harcourt Brace Jovanovich, 1929), pp. 43-44.
2. *A Room of One's Own,* p. 21.

so that professors and students would, rather than could, meet with each other as a matter of course, conveniently and daily. (This office space has since been reduced sharply.) The desire was not to provide luxurious accommodation, but to insure an environment with minimal distraction and maximum faculty-student conversation. But, as at many other colleges, two or three rooms originally intended for two students now host four, five, or six students, a telephone or two (often with attendant answering machines), several stereos and radios, and two or three television sets. For many students it is virtually impossible to sit privately in a small room and count on being able to read or write for several undisturbed hours.

Driven out of their housing in search of quiet and privacy, students do not always find a better environment elsewhere. In many college libraries a remarkable degree of conversation, chatting, and stage whispering is tolerated (the library is, after all, often regarded as a second—or only—social center). Some libraries provide superb study space and quiet; but others, unfortunately, are uncomfortable, poorly furnished and poorly lit, large and barn-like, with no one monitoring or enforcing any semblance of silence. Other problems arise. For instance, we want students to hear poetry, to read or recite it out loud, but the library is hardly the place for that, and without some privacy, the regular practice of reading poetry aloud to hear its music and chants and rhythms is sufficiently discouraged. In urban settings most rooms, dining halls, offices, and buildings, when not scheduled for regular use by groups, are locked to prevent theft or damage.

The American university is both curiously structured and highly fragmented in its scheduling. Probably no two students or faculty in any university have the same daily schedule; however, their schedules usually are filled, often in conflict. Not only are many terms too brutally short to digest and assimilate literary material (inevitably, in faculty wrangling over calendars, it is the humanists who argue against shorter and shorter terms), but weeks and days are segmented, scheduled, and "filled up" with a passion that often makes four or five free hours an event so unusual that it is understandably used to recover from the previous twenty-four or forty-eight. Time is sliced too thin for the mind to form itself. Most students take a full load of courses, lab work, and scheduled activities that together perforate the days of the week. While only part of their time is actually scheduled, it is scattered so thoroughly that any remaining time is even more scattered—the leavings only. Add to this a healthy interest in community service, voluntary activities, and sports (often requiring extensive travel), and a student may be fortunate to have several hours clear at a stretch. Moreover, many students must work ten to twenty hours a week to help pay for their education. Some subjects can survive or even flourish under these conditions of diced-up hours and days. Most technical or quantitative forms of knowledge can be absorbed in segments with little damage; this way of learning is even preferable in some instances. Lab work, even of long duration, is appropriately scheduled and the laboratory contains no distractions; there is usually a set procedure to follow that is self-directed, providing its own concentration.

As a result of increased scheduling pressures, newly generated and fluctuating with each term, the material that does not require weekly problem sets, rote memorizations, and technical mastery suffers under time-tables geared to serve these forms of learning and teaching. A faculty that must commute because proximate housing is hard to afford adds further strictures to schedules and meetings with students. In addition, the expanding administrative structures that oversee all university activities and personnel begin to exact their own toll. The more complex and larger the administration becomes, the more student (and faculty) time and energy are devoted to internal governance, and to satisfy bureaucratic requirements—either directly or indirectly—the professoriate and student body both become caught up in metaprocedures and superstructures.

The technological advances transforming the American university, so beneficial in revolutionizing the means and conditions of study in many if not most other fields, have so far exerted a limited impact on reading and writing. Word processing, microfilm, and computer library searches or databases are, of course, primary examples. But word processing and automated searches are time-saving devices used so that more time can be devoted to the very processes they speed, rewriting and thinking. Even without word processors and computerized library files (themselves compiled by all-too-fallible individuals often distinguished more for technical expertise than for close knowledge of the books they are filing), one could still rewrite or research, or make a concordance or index—it would simply take a modicum of extra time. By contrast, in many other fields computers perform (among other things) calculations, data analyses, or simulations that otherwise would be literally impossible in length and time consumed—hence not only is enormous time saved, but one can do something one could otherwise never do at all. In literature there are remarkably few instances of this. Authorial attribution on evidence of stylistic, vocabulary, and syntactic patterns may be one, but even there it is easier, usually less valuable, to establish that a particular author did not write the work in question than to prove who actually did. It is a specialized area, one which few literature majors explore.

In advocating student privacy, proper study conditions, sane scheduling, and an ability to escape distractions, I think it is important to note that providing such a temporary, secular cloister does not presuppose that exposure to the world of political, mercantile, and professional interests is somehow detrimental or inferior, but takes for granted that such exposure and all its responsibilities, choices, and pressures are inevitable and cannot be ignored: they soon arrive for the rest of life. But while the modern college, particularly the research university in an urban or exurban locale,[3] has grown superbly adept at providing this kind of exposure and training, and the accompanying physical and

3. Large schools eventually create their own city even if they were orginally suburban or rural in location. Letters sent to Stanford, Notre Dame, or the University of Alabama no longer are addressed to Palo Alto, South Bend, or Birmingham, but the city is replaced by the university name (simply "University" in the case of Alabama) and its own zip code.

technological requisites for professional studies, it often fails to guarantee the indispensable and minimal conditions for literary activity—that is, an available absence or exclusion of those requisites provided for most other disciplines. This entails a protection or creation of the kind of space and daily habit in the university landscape and structure that are most conducive to literary study. One might recall the several lines in *The Prelude* where Wordsworth speaks of his college room as "my abiding-place, a nook obscure," but his own, and of times he would read "For a whole day together" or contemplate "The hemisphere / Of magic fiction" alone, "Through hours of silence."

In the end, the requirements, broadly put, are space and time—in other words, money. Yet in the teaching and study of literature the results of investment rarely look impressive to the material eye or development office brochure; they are almost intangible: rooms devoted simply to reading and writing with comparatively little, if any, technology or equipment. To argue effectively for improvement in conditions for literary study is hard for teachers in disciplines constantly identified as ones that "bring in no money." The irony is that the very studies now often told this—*litterae humaniores,* philosophy, history, the study of languages, and theology—orginally created both the idea and the fact of the modern university.) What is not advocated here, and the last thing needed in the teaching of literature, is arbitrarily curtailing student and university activities or a jealous, competitive attitude toward other disciplines. But as teachers and students living and working in institutions, we require nothing more, and nothing less, than the ability to escape the conditions necessarily provided for most other studies, and to find solitary time in a room of one's own.

Literature has often treated its own decay in apocalyptic terms. *Fahrenheit 451, Brave New World,* and *Animal Farm* posit a decline or corruption in language and the liberating force of literature as a result of active censorship, tyranny, or political ideology. And certainly book burnings are painfully fresh in the minds of many living individuals. But in the American system of higher education, the present erosion in conditions for teaching, learning, and loving literature and language stems from a curious institutional evolution that, without intending to hamper literary studies, now threatens to undermine them precisely where those studies must take root for students, and where they must survive for their adult lives: outside the classroom.

As teachers, heads of departments, some-time administrators, committee chairs and members, and as voices in the college or university community, we need to secure an environment in which literary pursuits can thrive not only for faculty, but for students. Where these seemingly simple conditions (actually elusive and costly) are no longer available, their absence frustrates all teaching.

Contributors

HUGH KENNER, Andrew W. Mellon Professor of the Humanities at The Johns Hopkins University, has written extensively on literature of the modern period. His books include *The Pound Era* and studies of Eliot, Beckett, and Joyce.

HELEN VENDLER's book-length studies of individual writers treat Keats, Herbert, Stevens, and Yeats. Her reviews and essays on contemporary and modern poets are collected in several volumes, including *Part of Nature, Part of Us.* She is William R. Kenan Professor of English at Harvard.

HARRY LEVIN, Irving Babbitt Professor of Comparative Literature, Emeritus, at Harvard, is known for pioneering work on Joyce, Marlowe, the American Renaissance, Shakespeare, and French Realism. His essays appear in several collections, and his most recent book is *Playboys and Killjoys: An Essay on the Theory and Practice of Comedy.*

NATHAN A. SCOTT, JR., is William R. Kenan, Jr., Professor of Religious Studies at the University of Virginia. His more than two dozen books cover topics in literature and spiritual life. Lately he published *The Poetics of Belief: Studies in Coleridge, Arnold, Pater, Santayana, Stevens, and Heidegger.*

BARBARA JOHNSON, Professor of Romance and Comparative Literatures at Harvard, has written extensively on critical theory, pedagogy, and the application of theory to particular texts. Her most recent work is *A World of Difference.*

DEBORAH EPSTEIN NORD is the author of *The Apprenticeship of Beatrice Webb.* At Harvard she is a member of the committee on the Degree in History and Literature, and Associate Professor in the English Department.

J. HILLIS MILLER, Distinguished Professor of English and Comparative Literature at the University of California at Irvine, has written numerous studies of nineteenth- and twentieth-century fiction and criticism. Among his more recent books is *The Ethics of Reading,* which ranges from Kant to de Man.

DAVID PERKINS has published books on Keats, Shelley, and Wordsworth and recently completed his two-volume *History of Modern Poetry*. He is John P. Marquand Professor of English at Harvard.

ROBERT N. WATSON, Professor of English at the University of California at Los Angeles, has written on Shakespeare in *Shakespeare and the Hazards of Ambition* and has completed a study of Jonson's comic techniques.

JUDITH N. SHKLAR is John Cowles Professor of Government at Harvard. Her studies of political and legal thought include books on Hegel and Rousseau, as well as *Ordinary Vices*, an examination of values in private and social life.

GREGORY NAGY, Francis Jones Professor of Classical Greek and Professor of Comparative Literature at Harvard, has produced studies of Greek and Indic poetry and wrote about the hero in Archaic Greek literature in *The Best of the Achaeans*.

RICHARD MARIUS directs the Expository Writing Program at Harvard, where he is Senior Lecturer on English. He has published two novels, a study of Luther, and *Thomas More: A Biography*.

JAMES ENGELL is Professor of English and Comparative Literature at Harvard. His writings on eighteenth- and nineteenth-century English and German literature and criticism include *The Creative Imagination*.

All contributors have devoted a major part of their careers to classroom teaching at the college and university level.